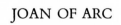

JOAN OF ARC

THE FIRST
BIOGRAPHY OF
JOAN OF ARC

With the Chronicle Record of a
Contemporary Account

TRANSLATED AND ANNOTATED BY

DANIEL RANKIN AND CLAIRE QUINTAL

UNIVERSITY OF PITTSBURGH PRESS

Headpieces for Provenance, Chronicle Comments, and Appendix are from a Latin Ms. of Joan's century, library of M. Ambroise Firmin-Didot. Those for Prologue, Biography Comments, and Booklists are from Chronicles of Monstrelet, who talked with Joan, No. 2678 Bibliothèque nationale. The one for the First Chronicle...is from Ms. fr. 189, Bibliothèque nationale. All were photographed from *Jeanne d'Arc,* H. Wallon. Coat of Arms of Joan of Arc is depicted here for the first time exactly as she described it during her trial. Drawn by Mrs. John Preston, Tryon, North Carolina.

To

Bishop John J. Wright

of

Pittsburgh in Pennsylvania

with gratitude and appreciation.

He has written eloquently

with genuine learning and gracious good humor

of

Joan of Arc

whose life, work, and sanctity

illustrate and illumine

the moral right

of

freedom of conscience

Bronze in St. Paul's Cathedral, Pittsburgh, Pennsylvania. Sculptor, Paul Shrady.

PREFATORY NOTE

It might well have seemed impossible to attempt the publication of yet another life of St. Joan of Arc unless, of course, one could come up with a translation of the first of all the hundreds of biographies of the Maid. That is what Father Daniel Rankin and Miss Claire Quintal decided to do; they then added, for good measure, a first English translation of a brief but eloquent (also anonymous) chronicle of great moments in Joan's career.

The latter document ends with the kind of words which have fired the determination of countless writers, musicians, and scholars to make the all but inaudible splash of the ashes of Joan in the Seine re-echo forever like thunder endlessly building up its reverberations. Commenting on the intensely practical wisdom of the British in shoveling the poor relics of the discredited girl into a bag to be thrown into the river, the anonymous chronicler observes that this was done "so that no attempt could ever be made, nor even a proposal be suggested, to use them for sorcery or any other mysterious evil."

Well, God save us from "mysterious evil," but preferably by the gentle, more enduring ways of knowledge and of love.

Father Rankin and Claire Quintal are the most recent to contribute to our knowledge of "the deeds and works of Joan who called herself the Maid." Their contribution is (quite beyond the work of translation) substantial, reasoned, erudite; it ranges from careful criticism of the history and value of some standard sources and of these new texts to intriguing bits of casual erudition for the sake of us less learned but deeply devoted partisans of St. Joan.

For example, how did the ill-fated Bishop Peter Cauchon spend the day after the cruel death that, as Joan reminded him, came to the saint through him? What kind of letters did Joan write and leave behind her, this girl who said of herself that she didn't know A from B? Precisely who taught a country girl tactical skill in the placement of artillery? What later became of those who appeared to have made out so well on the day that Joan clearly made out so badly?

These and like questions receive fresh, fascinating answers in the extensive notes added by the translators. It is in their commentaries that one senses not only the diligence but the great love of these latest scholars to have come to the service of Joan.

Both have done me the honor of confiding in me the separate and intensely personal backgrounds of the motivation of the love brought to this work and destined, one rejoices to know, in their projected further books on Joan. Their passionate partisanship breaks through with mild explosions from time to time in the authors' commentary. Should this irritate the bleakly dispassionate, let these be grateful that the same love gave origin and perseverance to the labor of making available two important documents and other rich material for the study of that life which Mark Twain dared to describe as the most noble life that was ever born into this world save only One. Mark Twain's praise is fulsome; it admits of debate. But Winston Churchill is not likely to be challenged in his assertion that "the ever-shining, ever-glorious Joan of Arc . . . finds no equal in a thousand years." Father Rankin and Claire Quintal clearly establish how early that fact was appreciated.

†John Wright
Bishop of Pittsburgh

CONTENTS

LIST OF ILLUSTRATIONS

THE FIRST BIOGRAPHY OF JOAN OF ARC

ABBREVIATIONS

Ay —Ayroles, J. B. J., *La Vraie Jeanne d'Arc,* 5 vols., Paris, 1890-1902.

Ch —Champion, P., *Procès de Condamnation de Jeanne d'Arc,* 2 vols., Paris, 1920-21.

D-L—Doncoeur, P. and Lanhers, Y., *Documents et Recherches relatifs à Jeanne la Pucelle,* 5 vols., Paris, 1952-1961.

T-L—Tisset, P. and Lanhers, Y., *Procès de Condamnation de Jeanne d'Arc,* Paris, 1960.

Q —Quicherat, Jules, *Procès de Condamnation et de Réhabilitation de Jeanne d'Arc,* 5 vols., Paris, 1841-49.

PROVENANCE

 UR WORK had its origin in a question prompted at times by interest at others by curiosity. We were asked frequently in England, France, the United States, and by friends from Sweden, "What was the *first life* of Joan of Arc?" or "Is there such a thing as a *first biography* of Joan?" The answer, we hope, is here. We make no pretense of a new discovery. The pages we have translated have been accessible for a long time to all who wished to take an interest in them, and some have. Our claim is a moderate one. We have moved this material out of its quasi-obscurity and placed it where it belongs—at the head of the long list of lives of Joan of Arc because it is the earliest in time. And we have added our *comments* on each section.

The anonymous author of this manuscript biography (and we believe this account of Joan of Arc's life is a biography) gives a clue to the time it was written. The author explains that he compiled the work "by order of the King, Louis XII of that name." This places the writing before 1515, which is the year Louis XII died. The eminent paleographer and historian Quicherat believed "it was written about the year 1500." The literary tone of the manuscript and its author's chirography belong to the early sixteenth century. To use a phrase of the distinguished and lamented

3

Professor C. S. Lewis: the style is characterized by "coupled synonyms."

It is French prose struggling away from the lack of individual style of the chronicles. The reader is left with the impression that the author is making an effort "to write better than he talked." He had a good story to tell and he is striving to tell it well.

Our translation has been done directly from Ms. fr. 518 in the Municipal Library of Orléans and from a contemporary fragment in a private collection. This first life of Joan of Arc was intended originally as an introduction or explanation to prepare the reader for Joan's trial of condemnation and a summarized account of her trial of vindication. Evidence is not wanting to prove that this life has had charm and popularity, not, of course, equal in interest to the record of the trials, but of sufficient appeal to be reproduced frequently both in manuscript and printed form. Ms. fr. 18930, *Chronique de Normandie*, in the Bibliothèque Nationale, dated "about 1522" by competent authority, incorporates part of Joan's life and sections of the trial of condemnation from the Orléans manuscript. Other variations of this *Chronique de Normandie*, for instance no. 1488 of the MSS of Saint Germain in the Bibliothèque Nationale, also use it. The title, "Abbreviator of the Trial," *(Abréviateur du Procès)* signifies the identical content so often borrowed.

This borrowing of the first life of Joan of Arc to add interest to the reissue of books already well received went on irregularly for more than a century. As will be indicated, the last reprint of the *Life* to increase the value of the contents of a book on Joan of Arc appeared in 1803 in Rouen. In that city the borrowings in print began. This permits the present translators to suggest that what is known today as the Manuscript of Orléans may have been written in

Louis XII (1462–1515), who commissioned this biography of Joan of Arc ca. 1500.

Louis Malet de Graville, Admiral of France (144?-1516), who persuaded Louis XII to have this biography written.

Rouen. Certainly, as internal evidence indicates clearly, the compiler of this first life writes as if he knew little of the English forts around Orléans at the time of the siege. He gives the impression of composing his account of the siege from incomplete information. Had he done his work in Orléans it is reasonable to expect a more detailed knowledge of the city. There is a remote possibility that he knew of the account Guillaume Girault, notary and twice municipal magistrate of the city of Orléans, wrote in his official record for 9 May 1429, where he enthusiastically recounts the glorious events of the preceding days, the deliverance of Orléans by Joan the Maid. That he may have been influenced by Girault's account is intriguing. (Boucher de Molandon, *Première Expédition de Jeanne d'Arc*, pp. XVI-XVII, 10).

⚜ ⚜ ⚜

A book in 16° published in Rouen before 1578 borrowed the manuscript life of Joan of Arc as part of its 38 pages. Its title page reads: "*Cy commence le Livre de la Pucelle: natifve de Lorraine, qui reduict France entre les Mains du Roy, ensemble le jugement et comme elle fust Bruslee au Vieil Marche a Rouen. Et a la fin plusieurs aultres choses advenues du depuys en la Ville de Rouen.* On les vend a Rouen au hault des degrez du Palaix, chez Martin le Mesgissier."

With a slight variation in the first sentence of the Rouen publication Joan is introduced as she is in the manuscript:

In the year one thousand four hundred twenty and nine there was in the land of Lorraine a young girl eighteen years or so of age called Joan, a native of the parish of Domremy. She was the daughter of Jacques d'Arc, a farmer, and she had never done anything else except watch over animals in the pastures.

This book lacks an indication of its exact date of publication. However, in 1578 the same editor republished his book in a slightly different format, 29 pages in octavo. The title, too, was shortened and improved. The volume's popularity is suggested by reprintings in 1581, 1589, and 1610.

It is curious and interesting to notice that this information about Joan of Arc, borrowed by a printer-publisher of Rouen, Martin le Mégissier, was annexed to his printing of a history, *Description du pays et duche de Normandye extraict de la Chronique de Normandye.*

The same thing happened in Orléans. The anonymous biography of Joan was added in 1611 to an edition of a book of history, *L'histoire et discovrs av vray du siege qvi fvt mis devant la ville dOrléans par les Anglois, le mardi 12 jour doctobre 1428 regnant alors Charles VII roy de France . . . avec la venue de Ieanne la Pvcelle . . .* , better known today as the *Journal of the Siege.* The editors and printers of this edition were booksellers of Orléans, Olyvier Boynard and his son-in-law Jean Nyon. The commercial value of this publication must have been rewarding. Interest in it spread far and wide through France. In 1619 a printer in Lyons, Claude Larjot, furnished readers there with his edition. 1621 was a banner year. Reissues were published in Orléans: two by Saturnin Hotot, another by Charles Roze, again another by Louis Foucault. During the same year printers in Rouen and Châlons issued their editions. French readers were being well supplied with information on the life of Joan of Arc, her trial of condemnation, and the siege of Orléans. Thus, her first famous achievements and her death were told in the narratives combined in one volume.

Readers in Rouen were treated to a new printing of the anonymous biography in a book published there in 1803 by Vincent and Philippe Guilbert. Theirs is a melange of material about Joan of Arc entitled, *Eloge historique de Jeanne d'Arc, surnommée la Pucelle d'Orléans, suivi de notes, de pièces justificatives, de son procès et de diverses remarques historiques.*

Except for the pages with a summary of the trial of vindication, J. A. C. Buchon published in Paris in 1827 and 1838 almost all the other sections of the Manuscript of Orléans, including its life of Joan, under the title *Chronique et Procès de la Pucelle d'Orléans.* This book and its title seem to have been the inspiration for a faked manuscript done by Henri Fabre of Lausanne (1829-91), who "indulged in fabricated manuscripts of special interest for French collectors." (Otto Kurz, *Fakes*, p. 85). Fabre invented his title, *Chronique de la Pucelle d'Orléans, Jehanne d'Arc.* His fabrication now reposes in the British Museum as Add. Ms. 30042, a reminder of bourgeois credulity. It is a stocky, ugly forgery, its "vellum thick as boards and just as hard." How anyone could have been duped by it is a mystery. In 1896 Albert Sarrazin in his *Jeanne d'Arc et la Normandie* (p. 4) accepted it as genuine.

During 1837, four years before Quicherat published the first volume of his now indispensable five-volume work, Michaud and Poujoulat edited a collection of documents entitled *Nouvelle Collection des Mémoires pour servir à l'Histoire de France.* Volume 3 reprints the anonymous first biography of Joan of Arc.

⚜ ⚜ ⚜

The first serious inquiry into the importance of the entire contents of the Manuscript of Orléans was made at the instigation of Clément Charles François de l'Averdy, who by royal permission sought out and evaluated all manuscripts relating to the trial of Joan of Arc. In volume 3 of his *Notices et extraits des manuscrits . . .* published in 1790 in Paris, he wrote an unfavorable judgment of the Manuscript of Orléans. He had neither examined nor read the manuscript. His opinion was based on the advice of others. Two scholarly priests in Orléans, Abbé Moutié and Abbé François Dubois, disagreed with him and upheld the special value of this manuscript. L'Averdy's superior position and prestige prevailed. In 1847 Quicherat included a portion of the first biography of Joan from the Orléans manuscript in his third volume, pp. 254-266. His volume five, issued in 1849, includes an estimate of the entire manuscript, pp. 411-418. Again the judgment is unfavorable. In 1872 Beckmann, the plagiarist of Quicherat, introduced German readers to the Manuscript of Orléans in his little book, *Forschungen über die Quellen zur Geschichte der Jungfrau von Orleans*, pp. 34-37. Pierre Champion accepted Quicherat's opinion as definitive in his *Procès de Condamnation* of 1920. Ayroles treats the subject in his volume 3, pp. 278-285.

⚜ ⚜ ⚜

The combined weight of authority represented by l'Averdy, Quicherat, and Champion awed students and readers into an acceptance of their hostile opinion. One scholar refused to be awed, the learned, genial Jesuit Father Paul Doncoeur (1880-1961). Amazed by the cavalier disregard of the arguments and conclusion of Abbé Dubois, he began a study of the Manuscript of Orléans. In 1952 he published the painstaking, persuasive results of his study, *La Minute française des Interrogatoires de Jeanne d'Arc*. His purpose was to indicate and establish the document's intrinsic value: its pages that deal with the trial of condemnation are the replies Joan gave in French to her Judges in answer to their questions. From what document did the compiler copy his material? From original records of the trial which are now lost. The omissions in the manuscript do not impair the validity of the argument. Father Doncoeur made no excessive claims for his own conclusions. His motive in all his research was to allot its proper importance even to the least detail in any document reflecting the speech and the opinions of Joan herself. Owing to Father Doncoeur's perception and judgment the Tisset-Lanhers edition of the *Procès de Condamnation de Jeanne d'Arc*, issued in 1960, includes the pages of the trial from the Manuscript of Orléans before 3 March 1431.

Since the original records of the trial were in Rouen and not in Orléans, Father Doncoeur agreed with our suggestion that the Manuscript of Orléans may have been compiled in Rouen. We wish to pay tribute to his stimulating friendship and to his constant, unselfish encouragement.

⚜ ⚜ ⚜

The anonymous author of this first biography compiled his life of Joan of Arc, as he explains, "by order of the King, Louis the XII of that name and of His Lordship Louis de Graville, Admiral of France."

The difficult problem of gathering information on Louis Malet de Graville is made less tedious as a result of the research published seventy-five years ago by P. M. Perret, *Notice biographique sur Louis Malet de Graville, Amiral de France, 144?-1516*. Almost unknown today, this admiral of France, "the last representative of an old and illustrious family of Normandy," began his public life of unselfish service under Louis XI. His most important work for the welfare of France was done under the regency of Anne de Beaujeu during the minority of Charles VIII. The affairs of the realm were in his hands. Today he would be called a Prime Minister whose wise and moderate policies at home and abroad kept the ship of state on an even keel. He was reputed fair and just. With his belief in the knightly quality of chivalrous honor, he devoted himself faithfully to the

9

interests of his young sovereign Charles VIII. His conscientious sense of public service was exceptional.

The title or distinction, Admiral of France, was given him during January 1487. At that time it did not demand, apparently, a skilled knowledge of seamanship. It seems to have allowed him to use his ability as a public servant in the capacity of a Secretary of Naval Affairs. One of his predecessors in this office in France, Louis de Culan, fought on land with Joan of Arc from Orléans to Paris.

The date of his birth is unknown. His biographer places it vaguely between 1441 and 1450. He died 30 October 1516. The accomplishments of his active life are spelled out and preserved in the array of his titles. His contemporaries agreed they were merited: Admiral of France, Lieutenant General for the King in Normandy, Governor of Picardy, Lord of Graville, of Montaigu, of Marcoussis, of Sees, of Bernay, of Vandeuil, Minister of War, Captain of Dieppe, of St. Malo, of Pont-de-Larche, Chevalier of St. Michel, and Governor of Paris in 1505.

He did not accompany Louis XII on his expeditions into Italy. At home he devoted himself to policies of benefit for the people at large. The Municipal Council of Rouen in 1493 proclaimed him "Father of the Country" (Pere du Païs). Like Washington three centuries later he was not influenced by selfish motives or personal interest. His ancestors delighted in the proud old Norman saying, "There was a Lord of Graville before there was a King of France." (Vulson de la Colombière, La Science héroïque, 1664, p. 159). Today what was Graville is part of the city of Le Havre.

The family's link of interest with Joan of Arc is Jean Malet de Graville, Louis Malet's grandfather, who is mentioned in many of the French and Burgundian chronicles. He shared with Joan of Arc the struggle for the deliverance of Orléans. He was at Jargeau, Patay, Reims, and Paris.

The distinctive position to which he was appointed in 1425 gave him the title of *Maître des Arbalétriers de France*, the Commander of the King's Crossbowmen.

⚜ ⚜ ⚜

Louis XII was the son of the poet Charles Duke of Orléans, detained after the disaster of Agincourt as a prisoner of war in England for a quarter of a century. During her trial on Thursday 22 February 1431, Joan of Arc mentioned this prisoner who was not to see France until 1440. The poet's father, Louis, Duke of Orléans, brother of Charles VI, had been assassinated in Paris in 1407. Bonne Visconti, a grandmother of Louis Malet de Graville, was the sister of Valentine Visconti, wife of the murdered duke. This relationship strengthened the ties between Louis XII and the Admiral. Joan of Arc had given back the city of Orléans to the Valois-Orléans family of whom Louis XII was the last representative.

⚜ ⚜ ⚜

Here we wish, with diffidence, to offer a conjecture— that Anne de Graville, one of Louis Malet's daughters, was the true instigator of this first life of Joan of Arc. There are two probable reasons. First, she was a writer. As Chaucer did long before her, she took from Boccaccio the story of Palemon and Arcita and rewrote it into a poetic version of her own. This is the most ambitious of her poems that have survived. Second, Anne de Graville, like Joan of Arc, was independent and determined, a woman of strong character and vigorous mind. Against the expressed will of her father she married her cousin, Pierre de Balzac. (*Anne de Graville* by M. de Laqueuille.) She named her own daughter Jeanne. This daughter brought to her husband Claude d'Urfé (1502-1558) a collection of books and manuscripts inherited from her mother. One of the treasures of this collection was the *Manuscrit d'Urfé*, designated today in the Bibliothèque Nationale as MS Latin 8838. It contains part of the French record of Joan of Arc's trial of condemnation. Quicherat annexed this section of the manuscript to his first volume in 1841. On his competent authority this was accepted as a transcript of the original minutes of the report of the trial until Father Doncoeur's authority granted the place of primacy to the report of the trial in the MS of Orléans. There is a curious interest in the realization that Louis Malet de Graville and his daughter Anne had both manuscripts to read. Champion was wrong about the significance of the MS of Orléans. We agree with him, however, when he writes, "C'est donc dans la maison de Graville que le translateur a travaillé." (Ch. I, XIV). The intellectural curiosity of a mind as vigorous as Anne de Graville's may have prompted her to propose a biography of the Maid. This unpretentious conjecture is expressed with the hope that further research will reveal conclusive evidence.

Daniel Rankin and Claire Quintal
Paris, April 28, 1964

Charles VII, for whom Joan saved France, pictured here in "his ceremonial hat of black velvet with ribbons of fine gold and three ostrich plumes in his own colors, white, red, and blue." Archives Nationales KK 53, f.28v.

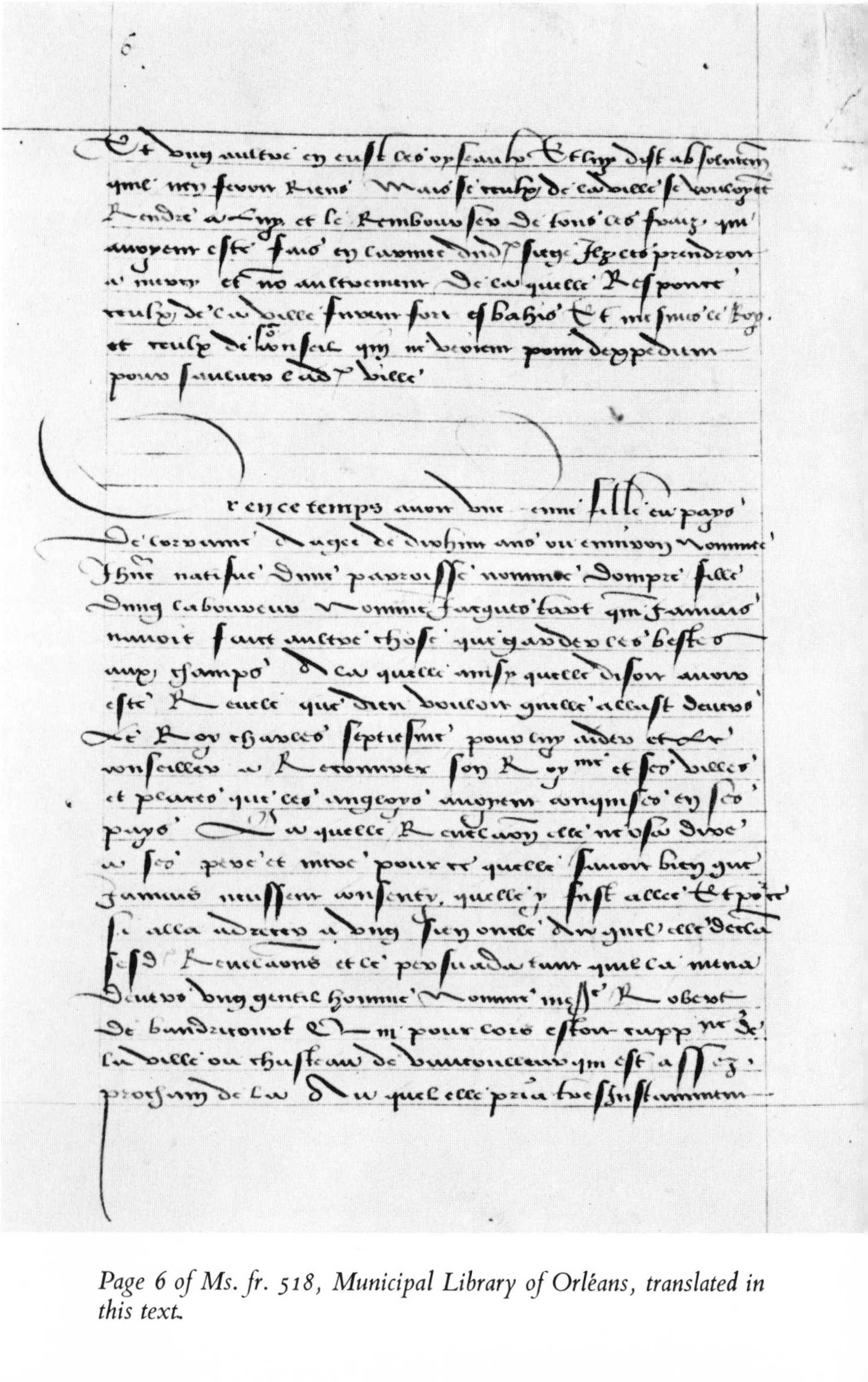
6

Et ung aultre en eust les oreilles. Et luy dist absolutement
que n'en feroit riens. Mais si ceulx de la ville se vouloyent
rendre a luy et le rembourser de tous les fraiz qui
avoyent este faiz en la armee dud. siege, il les prendroit
a mercy et non aultrement. De laquelle responce
ceulx de la ville furent fort esbahis. Et mesmes le Roy
et ceulx de son conseil qui ne veoient point de expedient
pour sauver lad. ville.

Or en ce temps avoit une jeune fille ou pays
de Lorraine, aagee de dix huit ans ou environ, nommee
Jehanne, native d'une parroisse nommee Dompre, fille
d'ung laboureur nomme Jacques Tart, qui jamais
n'avoit fait aultre chose que garder les bestes
aux champs. A laquelle avoit, ainsi qu'elle disoit, avoir
este revele que Dieu vouloit qu'elle allast devers
le Roy Charles septiesme pour luy ayder et le
conseiller a recouvrer son royaume et ses villes
et places que les Angloys avoyent conquises en ses
pays. Laquelle revelacion elle n'osa dire
a ses pere et mere pour ce qu'elle savoit bien que
jamais n'eussent consenty qu'elle y fust allee. Et pour ce
si alla adresser a ung sien oncle, auquel elle declara
ses revelacions et le persuada tant qu'il la mena
devers ung gentil homme nomme messire Robert
de Baudricourt, lequel pour lors estoit capitaine de
la ville ou chasteau de Vaucouleurs, qui est assez
prochain de la. Auquel elle pria tres instamment

Page 6 of Ms. fr. 518, Municipal Library of Orléans, translated in this text.

que se la fist mener devers le Roy de france de par
disant que estoit besoing et chose tresnecessaire quelle
parlast a luy pour ce bien de son Royaulme et
que elle luy feron grant secours et ayde a recouvrer
sond[?] Royaulme et quelle luy feroit grant sec[ours]
et que dieu le vouloit ainsi et que se luy avoit este
Revelé et quil luy avoit este Revele par pluseurs foys
Desquelles paroles Je ne fusson que Rire et se moqro
Et len Reputoit comme fransec[?] Toutesfoys elle proc[?]
tant et si conquement quil luy baillo ung gentil homme nom[é]
ville Robert Et quelque nombre daultres gens esquelz
la menerent devers le Roy [Or?]m pour lors estoit
a chinon Et ou quel lieu elle fut presentee aud[it] seigne[ur]
Et si tost quelle fut entree en la chambre ou se estoit
elle fist ces Inclinacions et Reuvences acoustumez a
faire aux Roys Ainsy comme se toute sa vie eust
este nouvrye en court Et apprez ce quelle Inclinacions
et Reuvences elle adressa sa parolle au Roy
Et quel elle ne avoit jamais veu et [luy?] dist dieu
vous donne bonne vie tresnoble Roy Et pource que
en la compaignie y avon pluseurs seigneurs vestus
aussi Richement ou plus que luy dist Si ne suis
pas ung suis Roy Ihne Et en luy monstrant quelque
[au?] seigneurs qui estoyent la presens Ludist Roy en
qui est Roy A quoy elle Respondu Cest vous qui
estes Roy Et non aultre Je vous cognoys bien
apprez ce quelles paroles Le Roy en fist
demander qui ca movoit a venir devers luy A quoy
elle Respondu quelle venoit pour lever le siege dorlens
et pour luy aider a Recouvrer son Royaulme

Philip the Good, Duke of Burgundy, an ally of the English.

PROLOGUE

At the present time in France princes and nobles, the lords and the people interest and concern themselves with the deeds and works of Joan who called herself the Maid. But they dispute and argue. The chronicles differ and disagree and many [people] of varied opinions discuss this interesting question *(font discussion de cette bonne matere)*. Each side obstinately insists on its own firm opinion. There is little chance of agreement and peace. *(Et tant sont obstines l'un contre l'autre que nul n'y peut mectre paix et concorde.)*

Some accept and approve what she said and affirmed, namely, that all the work she did was by command of God. Others speak of her serious errors against faith, how she cast wicked spells and how when the evil she did was pointed out to her she was neither penitent nor repentant. These argue, "For this reason she was judged by the law to die *(jugee a mourir)* and then burned to death in the city of Rouen for her misdeeds *(en la ville de Rouen pour ses demerites)*."

My reply to them is, "She was condemned and executed, but unjustly and through hatred, as is shown clearly in [the records of] her trial of condemnation as well as that of her vindication, both of which I will write out later on." Then all who read will see and realize without difficulty how dishonest and unjust were her condemnation and death, and what part hatred had in both.

I write this by order of the King, Louis the XII of that name, and of His Lordship Louis de Graville, Admiral of France.

To all who may read [what I have written] my prayer is, "Please bear with me, the writer, and forgive me for the mistakes and inaccuracies you may find."

When I had examined and read all the chronicles which we call the Great Chronicles of France with those by Froissart and Monstrelet and Gaguin as well as several compiled by other writers, I then considered and compared carefully all the marvelous happenings in [the history] of the kingdom from the days of Marchomire and Pharaon, the sons of the first king of France, right up to the present time. I found no event so remarkable or memorable [as the story of Joan of Arc], nor one more deserving to be written down and to be kept as a lasting memory by the French. In short [I write this] so that the kings of France, her princes and her lords, her nobles and all the people of this country may appreciate and interpret the remarkable favor God has manifested by saving them from falling into the servitude and sinking into the subjection of the old enemies of France, the English.

I

THE ENGLISH LAY SIEGE TO ORLÉANS

In the days of King Charles VII during that year of favor, one thousand four hundred twenty and nine [1428], after the before-mentioned English had made several conquests and seized and held under their obedience and control all the cities and regions of Normandy, Picardy, Champagne, Maine, Anjou, Touraine and Beauce, and broadly speaking, all the territory [of France] down to the river Loire, the Earl of Salisbury and William de la Pole, the Earl of Suffolk, with Sir John Talbot and sundry lords and captains of England accompanied by a large number of men-at-arms proceeded to subject Orléans to a siege. They aimed at capturing it to provide themselves with a passage across the river Loire for their advance into the territory of Berry and Auvergne and other areas beyond, even as far as Lyons.

To direct the siege more securely they built there four stout fortresses, two on the Beauce side and two on the Sologne side of the city. These they fortified with moats, artillery, and other necessary means [of defense]. In this way the English held the city in so strong a subjection and caused its inhabitants such dire distress they were unable to receive food or relief without serious trouble and danger.

The English persisted for so long a time in this siege that no matter what measures the King [Charles VII] resolved to take to help those [in Orléans] with provisions and soldiers, they were in such dreadful need that they had hardly any hope of their ability to hold out against the enemy.

The captains and soldiers inside the city realizing they could not obtain food without disastrous risks and damage —because they had very little prospect of help from the King—and understanding that the people of the city had not the least intention of falling under the authority of the English or being subject to them, summoned the principal citizens and merchants of the city and pointed this out to them:

We have no way to provide the city with food unless we take a risk fatal for us all. We do not see any means of holding out against the enemy. We do not have the least hope, none at all in fact, of help from the King. Therefore, we ask you to tell us what you want us to do!

The decision was unanimous: "We will not submit to the subjection of the English! We will die first!" Then the captains remonstrated further, "Do you realize the danger we are all in?" The citizens remained steadfast in their determination, "We will not surrender the city!"

✤ ✤ ✤

After this decision several proposals were made about means to find some expedient for the good of the city. Finally everyone agreed to accept this plan or project:

We will send to the Duke of Burgundy, who now sides with the English, asking him to be willing to take us under his protection for we will be happy to give up our city to him. It is best to do this because the Duke is related to the Royal House of France. We firmly believe that the present alliance between him and the English will not last forever.

To carry out their intention the citizens dispatched a captain by the name of Poton de Saintrailles to the Duke to present their proposal to him. He gave it his approval, on one condition: "Provided that the Duke of Bedford who commands the English besieging Orléans is willing to give *his* consent."

The Duke of Bedford had come there after the death of the Earl of Salisbury, killed by accident, as the story goes, by a "piece of artillery" while directing the siege on the Sologne side. As it is clearly stated in the Great Chronicles, "No one knows who touched the flame to that piece of artillery."

Poton, whom I have mentioned went on to the Duke of Burgundy. When the Duke of Bedford heard the proposal made to the Duke of Burgundy, he retorted,

I did not beat the bushes for game to have someone else get the birds. I'll have none of it! But if the people of Orléans decide to surrender to me and will reimburse me for all the money expended on our army during the siege, I will grant them quarter. Otherwise, nothing!

This extreme ultimatum astounded the inhabitants of Orléans, and even the King Charles VII and his Council, for all were at a loss for an expedient to save the city.

JOAN OF ARC MEETS CHARLES VII

But there was at this time in the land of Lorraine a young girl eighteen years or so of age called Joan, a native of the parish of Domremy. She was the daughter of Jacques d'Arc, a farmer, and she had never done anything else except watch over animals in the pastures. To her, as *she* said, the will of God had been revealed.

I must go to the King Charles VII to advise and help him recover his kingdom as well as the cities and fortresses conquered by the English in his domains.

She dared not tell this revelation to her father and mother for she knew they would never assent to her going to the King. For this reason she went and appealed to an uncle of hers to whom she made known the revelation I have mentioned. She had such a power of persuasion that he took her to a man of gentle birth by the name of Sir Robert de Baudricourt, at that time captain of the town and castle of Vaucouleurs quite near Domremy. Joan begged him insistently to arrange for her to go to the king of France. She explained,

There is a need—it is a matter of serious necessity—for me to speak to Charles VII for the benefit of his kingdom, and bring him important aid and help for the recovery of his realm, important help, I repeat, for it has been revealed to me several times, that God wills it!

At these words he did nothing but laugh at her and make fun of her. He thought her flighty. However, she persisted steadily and for so long a time that he yielded and provided her [with an escort], a gentleman by the name of Ville Robert and a small number of other attendants, who took her to the King at that time in Chinon, where she was introduced to the monarch I have already mentioned.

When she came into the room where he was, she immediately made the inclinations and reverences one is accustomed to make to kings, exactly as if all her life had been nourished at court.

After these inclinations and reverences she spoke to the King whom she had never seen before and said, "May God give you a good life, very noble King!"

Because in that assembly several lords were dressed as richly or more so than he, the King replied, "But I am not the one who is king, Joan."

Then as he pointed to one of his lords among those present he said to her, "There, over there, is the one who is King." To this she replied, "You are the King and no one else. I recognize you indeed!"

After these words the King asked her this question, "What prompted you to come to me?" She explained, "I have come to raise the siege of Orléans and to aid you to recover your kingdom. God wills it so." She continued, "After I have raised the siege I will conduct you to Reims to be consecrated. Do not distress yourself over the English, for I will combat them in any place I find them."

Then she concluded, "Give me as many fighting men as you can afford to pay, for I have no doubt about doing all these things, even driving the English out of your kingdom."

⚜ ⚜ ⚜

At this point the King had questions put to her about faith. She was queried on several other matters, namely, on things holy, on war, and other subjects of equal interest.

She answered all questions with such intelligence that the king, the bishops, and the priests who were present were astonished, and not without reason, when one considers the simplicity and the occupation of this girl who had never done anything except watch over animals in the pastures.

⚜ ⚜ ⚜

At the conclusion of these questions and answers that I speak of, the King called together the members of his Council who recommended that Joan be asked again what she planned to do. Her reply was, "To make war on the English and to raise the siege which is now blockading Orléans."

For this reason she implored the King to dispatch one of his armorers or another individual to Saint Catherine of Fierbois.

I want whoever goes there to bring back to me a sword which he will find in the church, in a particular place which I will describe to him. Fleurs-de-lys are cut into this sword, five on each side.

Then someone asked her, "Were you ever in the neighborhood of St. Catherine?" She replied, "No, but I know by divine revelation that this sword I speak of is in the church. It is there in between several pieces of old scrap iron." As she turned to the King she added, "With this sword and the help of God and that of my good captains and soldiers, I will raise the siege of Orléans and accompany you to Reims where you will be consecrated and crowned, exactly as the Kings of France, your predecessors, have always been crowned."

After this declaration the King was urged to send one of his armorers to St. Catherine of Fierbois. [The one sent] readily found the sword spoken of and fetched it to the King who presented it to Joan the Maid. She very humbly thanked him for it and requested him to give her a horse, armor, a lance, and other equipment required for war. All these things were straightway delivered and given to her.

She accepted them at once, had the armor put on, and immediately mounted the horse and poised her lance as in a joust. In all details she acted like a man and a soldier, as one born to the ways of war.

Moreover when she was invited to the King's Council there to give advice and to deliberate on what to do, whether to raise the siege of Orléans or to recover towns and fortresses or to venture on an enterprise against the enemy, she spoke and debated so shrewdly and sustained her opinions with arguments so convincing that very often against the judgment of the captains her opinion on what they were to do was followed. And what is even a greater wonder, if the King and his Council held a meeting in her absence, she knew all they had discussed and decided, the same as if she had been there. The King and his associates were much amazed at this. Well they might be!

Even though the chronicles I have read do not make mention of one detail which I heard told and repeated long ago, not merely once but many times, by eminent people of distinction in France, who asserted they had read this particular fact in well-authenticated chronicles, and even though [I have not read it] I have duly resolved to add it here to what I am writing, on the one hand on account of the prestige and good repute of those who told it to me and, on the other because, in my opinion, it is a matter *worthy of remembrance.*

This is the account as I recall it.

After the King heard what the Maid said, his confessor or someone else made this recommendation, "In order to have more confidence in Joan and to settle [the question] of faith and belief in her words, talk to her in secret and

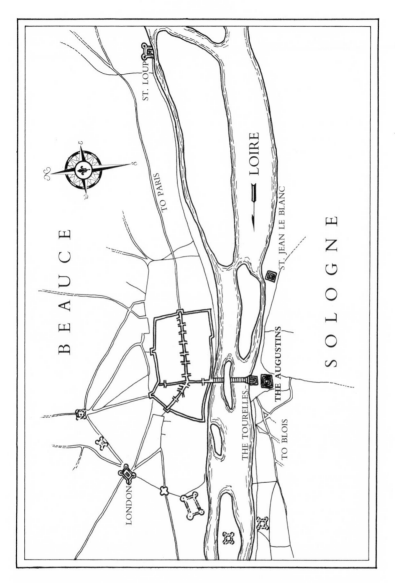

Map 1. Orléans during the siege with the English fortresses named by the author of this first biography. (Other English forts not named are outlined.)

Preparing to fire a fifteenth-century bombard.

find out how she can have such positive assurance that she is sent to you by God."

This the King did. To his question she replied, "Sire, if I tell you things so secret that no one but you and God know them, will you truly believe that I have been sent by God?" The King answered, "Yes." The Maid went on, "Sire, do you not remember how on last All Saints Day, all alone in the oratory of your chapel in the castle of Loches you made three prayers of petition to God?" The King said, "Yes, I am well aware of the three requests." The Maid inquired further, "Have you told or revealed these requests to your confessor or anyone else?" The King answered, "No!" "Then," Joan said, "if I tell you the three, will you believe my words?" Again the King said, "Yes." Whereupon the Maid told him, "Sire, your first prayer was this. Because you no longer wanted to be the cause of making and continuing war, the source of so many woes, to regain your kingdom, you said this prayer: *'Oh, God, let it be your pleasure to make me lose heart in pursuing [my heritage], if I am not the rightful heir of France.'*

"In the second prayer you begged God, *'If I am the cause of the heavy afflictions and calamities which the poor people of France endure and have endured for so long or if my sins are their source, let it be Your pleasure to lift them from the people and inflict them on me alone. Let me carry the guilt even unto death or any other chastisement according to Thy Holy Will.'*

"Your third prayer was, *'May God pardon the people, if their sins are the cause of these afflictions. I appeal to You to appease Your anger willingly and to release this kingdom from the misery it has known for a dozen years or more.'* "

The King admitted she knew the truth and with faith in her said, "I believe God has sent you and I have great hope that you will help me regain my kingdom." The King in his own mind carefully considered the question of accept-

21

ing her assistance and of putting faith in her counsel for all his affairs.

3

CHARLES VII SENDS JOAN TO BLOIS
FOR SUPPLIES TO RELIEVE ORLÉANS

Now it is time to come back to my theme.

The King, realizing the grave need for speedy relief to those under attack in Orléans, summoned his Council—to which Joan was likewise called—to weigh the means of [bringing] assistance and sustenance to those who were under siege. "I will undertake to do both, if you give me armed men," was Joan's declaration.

Then the King took further counsel with his captains. They, knowing and admitting the dire necessity of those besieged, the resolute success of the English, who, up to that moment, had achieved their aim in all their projects, and the extremities in which the affairs of the King and the kingdom existed, were of the opinion that the King might make use of this proposal of the Maid.

All agreed to do this.

Gilles de Rais and Ambrose de Loré were assigned to accompany and escort her. They traveled with Joan to Blois where she was received with due honor by the Chancellor of France, Regnault de Chartres, Archbishop of Reims, the Bastard of Orléans, La Hire, Poton de Saintrailles, and other captains, all of whom were in the city. With all diligence they took such steps as were required to provide the ordnance and supplies needed in Orléans, that is to say, stores, four-wheeled wagons, two-wheeled carts, horses and everything else required in such a situation. During the time taken to accumulate the equipment I have mentioned, the Maid wrote a letter to the King of England, the Duke of

Bedford, and other notables and military leaders of that country. Here is the letter.

JESUS, MARY †

KING OF ENGLAND and you, the Duke of Bedford, who declare you are the Regent of the realm of France; and you, William de la Pole, Earl of Suffolk, and you Sir John Talbot, and you Thomas Lord Scales, who say you are the Lieutenant of this Bedford, render an account to the King of Heaven! Give up to the Maid, who is sent by God, the King of Heaven, the keys of the cities you have seized and violated in France. She has come here, by God's order, to reinstate the royal line [of Charles VII]. She is fully prepared to offer [terms of] peace, if you are willing to give satisfaction, provided you agree to vacate France, settle the claims for the damage you have done, and repay the sums of money you have taken during all the years you have occupied this realm.

To you, archers, fellow soldiers, men of gentle birth, and all others who are in front of the city of Orléans, [I say] by God's order, GO HOME TO YOUR OWN COUNTRY. Unless you do, be prepared for further orders from the Maid who in a short time is going into action [against you]. You will suffer very heavy damage.

KING OF ENGLAND, I am a military commander and unless you accept my counsel, this I assure you: in whatever region of France I find your troops I will give battle and chase them and make them flee this country whether they want to or not. If they do not obey, I will have them all slain. I have been sent here by command of God, the King of Heaven, to combat them and boot them entirely out of France. If they obey willingly, I will show them mercy. And for you, do not make up your mind to remain here, for God, the King of Heaven and Son of the Virgin Mary, has given you no authority over this kingdom of France. Charles [VII], the RIGHT-FUL HEIR, will have this authority. God, the King of Heaven, wills it! The Maid has revealed to him that before long he will take possession of Paris in good and glorious company.

If you are reluctant to believe this communication [written] by the command of God and the order of the Maid, I caution you: in whatever place we encounter you, we will give battle and strike you down. There we will make a boisterous outcry (*hayhay*), the like of which has not been heard in France for a thousand years. Have a firm faith [in what I say]. The King of Heaven will give such power to the Maid that neither you nor your armies will know how to injure her or the troops she commands. When it comes to might, we will see who has the better right!

Duke of Bedford, you who now carry on the siege before Orléans, the Maid implores you not to force her to destroy you. If you do give satisfaction to her, you may yet live to see the French perform the most brilliant exploit ever turned to the account of Christianity.

If you wish to restore peace, I pray you to make reply in the city of Orléans which I hope to reach in a short time. If you do not act in this wise, you will ever bethink you of your heavy loss [of soldiers in battle].

WRITTEN THIS TUESDAY OF HOLY WEEK
[22 March 1429].

⚜ ⚜ ⚜

The March to Orléans

With preparations made to start out for the relief of Orléans, Joan the Maid, in the company of the Bastard of Orléans, Gilles de Rais and Ambrose de Loré, La Hire, and Robert de Baudricourt, newly arrived from Vaucouleurs, and other captains with a certain number of soldiers departed from Blois to escort the food and fodder made available. [The convoy] took the route on the Sologne side and Joan urged the whole group to make haste with all possible dispatch. When the English in their sturdy boulevard built at *Saint Jean le Blanc* were notified of the coming of the French, they abandoned their boulevard and withdrew into *The Augustins* which they had powerfully fortified.

The Maid, aware of the enemies' withdrawal, had all the supplies pass on in front of them and with all possible speed had these provisions stowed into barges and ferried across the river. This done, she and her entire escort with their own provisions crossed over the river into the city, where they were greeted with joy.

❦ ❦ ❦

On the morrow as soon as Joan and the lords and captains whom I have mentioned became aware that the supplies they had convoyed would suffice only a few days, they reached a decision to send [an appeal] back to Blois to the Chancellor, the Archbishop of Reims—I mentioned him before—to provision the city anew. For this purpose they dispatched the Bastard of Orléans, Gilles de Rais, and Ambrose de Loré with their escorts to explain again the exigency of those within the city. They were to say, "If you do not give us aid without delay, we will be forced to surrender the city to the enemy!"

In the meantime Joan the Maid waited in Orléans with other captains and soldiers to renew the courage of those within the city and to help them ward off an attack, in case the enemy decided to make every effort to carry it by storm.

When the Bastard, de Rais, and de Loré made their appeal to the Chancellor and others of the King's Council who were there at hand, an order was given to provide an impressive amount of food and provender. This was done immediately. Then the decision was reached to take these supplies to Orléans along the route through La Beauce.

The moment this materiel was brought together, the

Bastard, de Rais, and de Loré, with all the men at arms they could muster, marched out of Blois at once along the route agreed upon, by way of La Beauce. With these provisions in their charge, they pitched their camp halfway along the road between Blois and Orléans. Very early in the morning of the next day they decamped and continued on the march until they reached a little village close to Orléans. The Maid, apprised of their approach, had all the captains and soldiers in the city mustered for an immediate sortie. She disposed her men in such good order that she and the troops marched out in front of the enemy who did not sally forth from their fortresses. And so they moved forward without hindrance and went on to join those who were bringing up the supplies. When they joined their forces and made certain of their strength, they marched back toward Orléans with the stores and passed again in front of the forts with no opposition and went into the city.

4

ORLÉANS DELIVERED

At this point the reader should realize that the English had built two solid forts on the Beauce [or North] side of the city. One, because it was larger and stronger, was called *London*. The smaller was named *Saint Loup*. On the Sologne [or South] side they built two others, one at the head of the bridge [*The Tourelles*], the other on the site of *The Augustins*. They had constructed a boulevard, as I have said, at *Saint Jean le Blanc*.

Next morning, Joan the Maid in full armor, with the nobles, the captains, and the soldiers prepared for battle. She sallied forth the first from the city and dashed on ahead to attack the fort of *Saint Loup* just mentioned. When the English in the stronger fort [*London*] saw this vigorous assault against their own people, they rushed out of their stronger fort to go to the aid of their own soldiers, but, righteously repulsed by the French, they were compelled to retreat into their own fortress. Whereupon the French renewed their attack more boldly and took *Saint Loup* by assault. All those within were either captured or killed. The Maid ordered the immediate destruction of the fort before she turned with her troops and rode back to Orléans.

The next day and for several days after, the nobles and captains met together several times for a number of secret parleys to discuss a possible attack on the fort called *London*. The Maid was not summoned to these deliberations. Finally they agreed to the attack as a feint. "In our estimation," they concluded, "the English on the Sologne side will dash across the river to aid *London*. This move will deprive these bastiles and forts of their garrisons. In this way we can capture the Sologne forts with a handful of our soldiers."

After this decision they deliberated about telling the Maid, to find out if she thought their idea to assault *London* was a good one. Her reply was,

You believe, gentlemen (*messeigneurs les cappitaines*) that because I am a woman, I do not know how to conceal a secret. For your information I know every detail you have discussed. Here I give you my pledge—I WILL NEVER REVEAL PLANS WHICH ARE TO BE KEPT SECRET.

After this declaration they decided the Bastard of Orléans, who knew her best, should detail their scheme to her. When he did, the Maid had this to say, "I agree with your plan, if it could work out as you foresee. However, because I am sure it will not, I do not approve."

This is why the nobles and captains did not dare make a move to carry out their project in opposition to her decision. In particular they reflected, "All things she has undertaken have been brought to a happy ending." At once

27

then they went on to ask her, "What are we to do?" She had an answer. "I think it wise to assault the forts in the vicinity of Saint Laurent on the other side of the river [the Beauce side]." They came to an agreement to do this.

⚜ ⚜ ⚜

Now there was a goodly number of boats moored to the walls of the city. The soldiers she wanted to take with her went aboard and all crossed the river, she with them, to the other bank. With sure dispatch she drew them up in formation to attack one of the forts. At her command they marched toward the one at the entrance to the bridge. [This was *The Tourelles*.] Entrusting herself to God she began the assault boldly. The fierce defense by the enemy prolonged this assault until about an hour before the sun set. Realizing the determined resistance of the enemy the Maid gave the signal of retreat to her troops who, on her order, withdrew toward the boats in which they had crossed the river. The English, seeing the French in retreat, charged out of their fort to reach the French as they attempted to draw back [to their boats], as I have said.

The Maid, on perceiving this, rallied her soldiers in good order to counter the onset. She inspired them with such strength of courage that they forced the English to waver and move back into *The Augustins*, against which she directed this new attack. In spite of the fort's superiority in artillery and manpower she took it by storm. The enemy was constrained to flee into the bastile [*The Tourelles*] which, as I have said, was at the head of the bridge. This fort had very strong towers of stone.

After this she detailed the lookouts for the night.

⚜ ⚜ ⚜

The next morning at dawn she gave the order of the day.

Soldiers, the time has come to storm the enemy. Today I give you my pledge that the English will be conquered and chased out of the Kingdom of France.

Joan's pledge animated the French with greater courage. Under its incentive they stormed the bastile which, I assure you, was defended by the enemy with determination. Undaunted by this resistance the French, cheered on by the words of the Maid, who was always in the forefront of the attack, did not decrease their efforts.

Joan, wounded in the leg (some say in the shoulder) by an arrow from a crossbow, without seeming to pay any attention to it, did not retire from the fight but gave an example of courage to her troops, who, following her example, leaped after her into the moat of the bastile. Aided by ladders which had been placed to project above the walls they entered within. This is how they took *The Tourelles* by assault!

From four to five hundred English were killed there, among whom death took three of their captains, Lord William Moleyns, Lord Richard Poynings, and Captain William Glasdale, officers who were in command of the siege on the Sologne side. All the others were captured. The English across the river on the other side [in Beauce] were witnesses of the assault and the capture of those taken but were powerless to come to their relief.

With this task accomplished the Maid and her company crossed over the bridge and reentered the city exactly as she had promised on her departure the day before. To celebrate the victory the inhabitants of Orléans started to sing the *Te Deum laudamus*. The church bells in the whole city rang out. All night long the citizens in high glee made merry noise. Next day in the early morning the enemy, understanding the menace that beset them, withdrew from the other forts and retreated in great haste to Meung. In

29

this way at last to the deep shame, damage, and embarrassment of the English the city was delivered from the suffering of the siege. To the King, his friends, and his subjects this was a matter of high honor and of great glory.

5

JARGEAU

[At this point in his narrative the compiler omits all mention of Joan of Arc's activities during the month between the fall of Orléans and the assault on Jargeau. A brief summary of her journeys during these weeks will supply this omission. Most biographers of Joan, in retelling the happenings of this month of journeys back and forth over a region today aptly called the "Route of the Castles in the Valley of the Loire," forget and fail to remind their readers that half of these weeks were taken up with Joan's convalescence. She was recovering from the damage and discomfort of the injury inflicted by the arrow

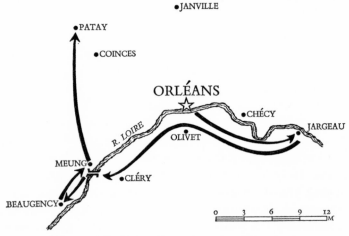

Map 2. The Loire Campaign 11–18 June 1429.

30

that hit her. We know from Joan's own words that the wound took two weeks to heal, although she did not stop riding horseback or doing her work. Her work, done with determination, was diplomatic. She had to persuade and convince Charles VII of the advantages of "the campaign of the Loire" and of the imperative need of going to Reims for his coronation. The King up to this time had made one rapid decision in his life. Years earlier, insulted by rude and scoffing remarks shouted as he passed by, he ordered, on the instant, the destruction of the castle of Azay-le-Rideau. Now, cautious and wary, his decisions were slow. Joan had to brave a monarch's sluggishness. This was her work. The days were not idyllic.

As will be seen, in the testimony of Simon Beaucroix, from Orléans Joan went to Blois. The *Chron. de la Pucelle* and Beaucroix indicate she moved from Blois to Tours. Then she went south to the castle of Loches, as Dunois and Beaucroix remember. On Saturday 4 June she was at "Selles-en-Berry," today Selles-sur-Cher. An item in the city treasurer's accounts for Orléans records a payment made to the herald, Jacquet Compaing, for a journey to Selles where he talked to Joan on 4 June, "le quatriesme jour de juing." (Q 5, 262). The young Laval brothers wrote a letter to their mother that confirms this account. They met Joan with the King near St. Aignan. From there the cavalcade moved to Romorantin (Q 5, 107). Another item in the financial records of Orléans indicates Joan was there again on Thursday 9 June. From Orléans she set out on Friday 10 June for Jargeau (Q 3, 94; D-L 5, 212).] *The Authors*

⚜ ⚜ ⚜

Now with the siege brought to an end, as I have said, the Maid entreated the King in earnest, "Assemble all the soldiers you can so that you will retake the cities and fortified places held by the enemy round about Orléans." For this reason the King gave an order to the Duke of Alençon: "REPORT BACK TO ME WITH ALL THE TROOPS YOU CAN MUSTER." This the duke did with diligence. Then he came to the

King with a great number of nobles and men-at-arms who, although they were to have no pay from the King, came nevertheless—at least the greater part of them—to see the Maid and to carry on the war in her company against the enemy. On all sides she was spoken of as—

ONE SENT BY GOD.

After the troops were inspected the army moved straight to Jargeau to subject the city to a siege. Eight days later through the counsel and skill of the Maid the city was carried by assault. Seized as prisoners there were the Earl of Suffolk, William de la Pole, with his brother [John]. Their other brother [Alexander] and very many of the English were killed.

6

MEUNG-SUR-LOIRE AND BEAUGENCY TAKEN FROM THE ENGLISH

After four or five days the nobles and their troops marched away from Jargeau, advanced to Meung, and there attacked and took the fortified tower at the entrance to the bridge and the bridge too. Then they posted lookouts in the tower, stationed their sentinels with great dispatch, and at once were on the march straight to Beaugency. Warned of the approach of the French the English evacuated the town and withdrew into the fortified castle which, two days later, they gave up by capitulation.

The Action at Patay

Not long after the surrender of the castle of Beaugency it was rumored about in the French ranks that Talbot and John Scales, at the head of five thousand English [troops], had reached Janville in Beauce, at that time under the authority of the English. Our forces were told that Talbot and his men were on the march toward Meung in the false belief that the French were laying siege to the place.

On hearing this news the [French] captains dispatched cavalry scouts to reconnoiter and report the reality of the situation. Their report was in these words, "Talbot is coming with a big army." As soon as this news came in the nobles and the captains held a meeting to ask the Maid's advice. She said, "In my opinion our entire French force must advance to encounter Talbot." They all replied, "Agreed!" We [the French] on our part ordered scouts out to determine the condition of the enemy. They reported, "The enemy is marching forward in regular formation." Then we decided to dispose our troops for battle.

First of all our advance guard was quartered in Patay, a village with a strongly fortified church. Sent out to ride with these were the Sire de Beaumanoir, Ambrose de Loré, La Hire, and Poton de Saintrailles with a goodly number of soldiers. The Duke of Alençon, the Constable [Richemont], the Count of Vendôme, the Bastard of Orléans, and Joan the Maid brought up the rear. When the English, trooping forward in order, caught sight of the French and saw their might, they veered toward a wood nearby to choose a field of battle more fit for combat. When our horsemen saw their maneuver to gain this wood, they smote them so rudely that the horsemen of our enemy were thrown into disorder and put to flight. The English foot soldiers, alarmed at the sight of their horsemen running away, scattered for safety into the woods and the adjacent village. But the Duke of Alençon in a rapid forward movement advanced into position, cut them down, and destroyed them. Three thousand and more of the English were killed there and several captains captured, Talbot among them.

After this disaster the village of Janville in Beauce and

other fortified towns close by returned to the allegiance of the King.

7

THE ROUTE TO REIMS

After these victories were won and the cities and fortresses I have mentioned were captured by the stratagem and skill of the Maid, she went directly to the King to say to him:

Beloved Sire, up to the present time, as you know, God, to Whom you should offer thanks, and your faithful servitors have cared for the interests [of your kingdom]. Now the time has come for you to begin to make preparations to go to Reims, where like the Kings of France, your predecessors, you will be anointed and crowned. It is God's pleasure that this be done. What a great benefit it will be for you! After the consecration, you, the revered, crowned King, will receive more

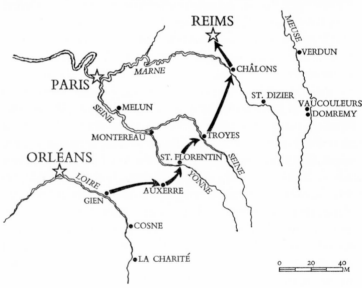

Map 3. The Route to Reims.

homage from the people of France. Your enemies will hold you in greater fear and dread. What if all the cities, castles, and fortified places along your route in Champagne are in the hands of your enemies? Have no anxiety. Aided by the power of God and that of your captains and soldiers you will move with safety along the way we will make for you. Assemble your soldiers. We will carry out the will of God!

Even after such words [of assurance] this venture impressed the King and his entire Council as very hazardous for, as it was said, "The entire province of Champagne has been seized by the English and is under their control." However, the Maid's confidence gave them a real hope of accomplishing what she was asking for, partly because she had achieved all her projects, partly on account of the upright and saintly life she led. They could see she went to confession very often and received the Body of Our Savior each week. Then again, they were aware that she never did any tasks [expected] of a woman.

After the Maid had had her say, as I have noted, the King went away to Gien on the Loire and summoned all those who could be of service to attend him on his march. Quite a number of those summoned came there to go forth with him and advance toward Reims. When decisions about details were settled, he gave immediate orders to several captains and their men-at-arms to move forward with the Maid to discover if the enemy were making preparations for combat. No time was lost in doing this. The captains and their troops took the route direct to Auxerre. The King and his army brought up the rear. When the people in the city of Auxerre learned of the King's approach, they showed such hostility—with the connivance of certain ones close to the King—that neither he nor any of his entourage entered that city. To the soldiers who paid for it, the inhabitants sold food. The King marched away and reached Saint Florentin. Here he was welcomed cordially. The people swore under oath to be loyal to him. Within a short time the whole army left this place and took the road to Troyes, a city which they besieged. After the King and his forces had spent six days in the assault, provisions for the troops failed. A new supply could not be found. This is why the fighting men were reduced to the necessity of having nothing except beans and kernels of grain for their food.

With starvation facing his army the King called together his nobles and captains, without bidding the Maid be present, for advice on what to do. With one exception their opinion was unanimous: the King should turn his army about-face and withdraw. First, because the troops lacked provisions; second, because the King had hardly any funds to pay his soldiers. Of those summoned to this Council all decided alike, except one by the name of Robert Le Maçon, who observed, "The views voiced here seem convincing enough, but I would be pleased to hear what the Maid has to say. She is the cause of this enterprise."

Presently the King had her summoned. The necessity of food for the army was explained to her. In view of the needs of the troops how was a new supply to be had? "In your opinion," asked the King, "what am I to do?" To this Joan replied, "Sire, if I tell you what I know to be the truth, will you believe me?" As the King did not answer promptly, she repeated her question. This time the King answered, "Joan, if you tell me anything to my advantage, I will readily believe you." Joan's words were, "I GIVE YOU, SIRE, THIS ASSURANCE. BEFORE TWO DAYS THE INHABITANTS OF TROYES WILL SUBMIT AND SURRENDER THE CITY TO YOU."

After these words were spoken the King was advised to delay [his departure] for two more days. He then issued an order, "No one is to withdraw from this siege." Immediately after this was proclaimed, the Maid, fully armed and mounted, had these words cried about through the ranks,

TO ALL MEN BEARING ARMS AND TO ALL OTHERS: Bring along scaling ladders, bundles of wood, tree branches, and other things we need [to aid] in assaulting the city.

She personally directed the casting [of the wood] into the moats and the position of the ladders against the walls. When they saw this, the city officials quickly authorized their bishop, with a group of citizens and a number of soldiers who were in the city, to go to the King. These agreed to surrender their city to him, if he consented to permit the English to depart in safety with their baggage. To this the King agreed and specified that on the morrow in the morning he would enter the city.

The next morning the English, taking with them some French [soldiers] whom they held as prisoners, were ready to set out safely from the city with their baggage. This the Maid would not tolerate! She then set the French prisoners free. The English protested, "This is an injustice! Contrary to the terms of capitulation!" Finally an agreement was reached. The prisoners were to be given their freedom, provided the King paid a certain sum of money as ransom. After this arrangement the King rode into the city where the people welcomed him right joyously and swore fidelity to him. He authorized [the appointment] of officials for the law courts and for the civil administration of the city. He had sentinels stationed to guard the place.

With this accomplished, the King set out and marched to Châlons where all the people greeted him with great joy and swore fealty to him. Here too he installed sufficient officials for the public welfare. Then he departed and went straight to Reims. Despite the fact that this city was under

English authority, its inhabitants acclaimed him with joyful enthusiasm and acknowledged him as their Sovereign Lord and King.

8

REIMS, THE CORONATION

The Dukes of Bar and of Lorraine and Robert of Commercy accompanied by an impressive number of men-at-arms came to Reims to present themselves to the King and offer their service to him. The King greeted them all, "I welcome you cordially and thank you for your noble good will."

Two days passed. [On Sunday, 17 July 1429] Charles VII was anointed and crowned by Regnault de Chartres, the

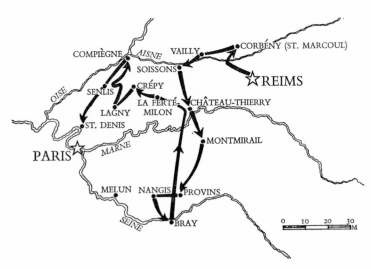

Map. 4. Reims to Paris.

Archbishop of Reims, in the presence of the Maid who bore the standard of the King in her hands. She rejoiced with great joy because by her entreaties and through her counsel and perseverance she had conducted the King to his consecration and crowning. She exhorted him to render thanks to God for the good he had received, for the honor the coronation was bringing him, and for the triumphs God had provided for him.

After the solemnities mentioned above and the oath of loyalty sworn by the people of the city, the King, following the Maid's suggestion, took his leave [of Reims] and proceeded on the road to Vailly-sur-Aisne, where he was readily received and acknowledged. It was exactly the same in Soissons. He moved forward from there through the province of Brie where he retook several fortified places held by his enemies. GOOD RESULTED FROM ALL THE ENTERPRISES HE VENTURED ON AT THE PROMPTING OF THE MAID.

9

CAPTURED AT COMPIÈGNE

Here I will refrain from adding further details to these actions and activities of Joan because all are related at full length in the chronicles I have mentioned. What I have selected to retell helps toward an understanding of the great deeds she did for France, for she is admirable and deserves to be remembered. I would not know how to relate and proclaim her exploits adequately. My intention is not and was not to retell them all in full detail.

Here I wish merely to relate how and in what way she was captured before Compiègne and afterward taken to Rouen. There her mortal enemies, the English, took strong legal action [against her] and the trial began. This court condemned her falsely and flagrantly to be burned to death, as the trial of vindication has since proved. This trial of vindication declared her innocent of all the charges in the accusation against her, in spite of the decision by the members of the University of Paris, who, sycophants as they were, to gratify the King of England, found her guilty of heresy, in opposition to the view of the late John Gerson, our Master, Doctor of Theology and the Chancellor of Notre Dame of Paris. His works show and prove that he

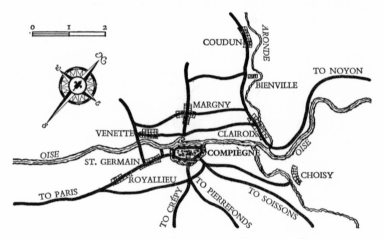

Map 5. Compiègne and Environs—the Siege of 1430.

was scholarly and judicious. At the end [of my book] I intend to include his opinion [of the Maid] with the arguments that brought him in opposition to the University. Thus the reader may decide on which side there is more likelihood of good sense and truth.

Now to come back to what I was saying about the Maid. Her renown spread more each day because the good fortune of the King flourished. He achieved without fail everything he did at her suggestion. Moreover she was given her share of appreciation and approval for all that was done. For this reason, as I have said, some nobles and captains conceived a great envy and hatred for her, something very likely and easy enough to believe in view of what was to happen before long. For while she was in Lagny-sur-Marne, she was told that the Duke of Burgundy and a goodly number of English had laid siege to the city of Compiègne, which a short while before had been brought under obedience to the King. With the few soldiers near her at the moment, she hurried from Lagny to bring help to those besieged within Compiègne. Her coming renewed the courage of the inhabitants.

A day or two later a sortie to attack the besieging forces was decided on by a certain number of those within the city. Although Joan did not approve the decision to make this sortie—as I have read in some chronicle—nevertheless she agreed to go out with this body of troops to avoid being thought a coward. This was her undoing. While she was bravely fighting off the enemy, someone among the French sounded the signal to retreat. Thereupon each one hurried to withdraw [from the combat]. Joan determined to retard the advance [of the enemy] to allow our troops time to retreat. When she herself came near the city gate, so many were forcing their way to it she found she could not get through. And there she was captured by the soldiers of John of Luxembourg, who was at this siege with the Duke of Burgundy.

Some prefer to say that one among the French was the cause of the hindrance that kept her from getting through the gate. This, though I will not say it is the truth, is easy for me to believe. Because it is not said [in the chronicles] that any other Frenchman, not even "a nobody," was captured or wounded at the gate. Be that as it may, [her capture] was a grievous injury to the King and his realm. You can judge of this by the astonishing triumphs and victories won in the short time she was with the King.

After her capture by the followers of John of Luxembourg, in the way I have explained, he had the Maid brought to his castle of Beaurevoir. In this place he took care to guard her very carefully day and night. He feared she might escape by magical trickery or some other subtle deception.

⚜ ⚜ ⚜

The King of England and his Council, alarmed that she might elude them through payment of ransom or in some other way, lost no time in laying claim to her. To uphold their demands [envoys] were sent several times to the Duke of Burgundy and to John of Luxembourg. The latter spurned their claim altogether. He would not listen to it.

At this the King of England was indignant. He convoked his Council for frequent discussions to hear their opinions. What was he to do to get possession of Joan? A conclusion was reached. Finally the King was advised to summon the Bishop of Beauvais to whom these facts were to be pointed out:

The Maid has made use of magic and diabolic cunning. She is a heretic. She was captured in your diocese. She is now a prisoner in your diocese. It is up to you to inquire into these matters. Summon and admonish the Duke of Burgundy and John of Luxembourg to hand over the Maid to you to bring her to trial as it is set forth in the provisions of the law of the Church against heretics. Offer to pay any reasonable sum agreed upon for her ransom.

After several protests the Bishop agreed to do this, with the proviso that his decision depended on the advice he received: could he and should he do it. He then appealed to the University of Paris to give him a legal opinion. He was advised, "You may and should proceed [with a trial]."

To court favor with the King of England, the University of Paris agreed with the Bishop's opinion that they should write to John of Luxembourg, who was keeping the Maid his prisoner, to release her to stand trial. Further, they would add, "If you do not you will prove you are not a good Catholic." Several other questions are treated in this letter, as will be seen in the copy which I will include further on.

As soon as the Bishop received the opinion and the proposal of the University he decided to forward such a claim, which was then put down in writing. Here follows
A TRUE COPY OF THE FORMAL DEMAND SENT BY THE BISHOP OF BEAUVAIS TO THE DUKE OF BURGUNDY AND JOHN OF LUXEMBOURG FOR THE DELIVERANCE OF THE MAID

By order of the King of England and under his own episcopal author-
ity the Bishop of Beauvais requires from the Duke of Burgundy and
John of Luxembourg and the Bastard of Wandonne
That this woman, the so-called Joan the Maid, now a prisoner, be handed over to the King of England who will transfer her to the Church. Under suspicion and reputed guilty of numerous crimes, she is to be charged with sorcery, idolatry, the invocation of demons, and other offenses, all contrary to our belief and against the Faith.
Owing to her evil reputation she is by no means to be dealt with as a prisoner of war. Nevertheless to reward those who captured her and who have kept her a prisoner, the King of England has decided to offer them [in exchange for her] a princely sum, not to exceed 6 thousand *livres*. To the Bastard [of Wandonne] who captured her, he proposes to allot an annuity in the amount of 2 or 3 hundred *livres* to [help him] maintain his estate.
Item. The Bishop, in his own name, calls upon those herein mentioned, individually and collectively, to consign this woman to him. As it behooves him, he will conduct the case against

her, for she was captured in his diocese and comes under his spiritual jurisdiction. He is fully prepared to assume this responsibility in association with the Inquisitor of the Faith. If the need arises [he is ready] to assemble doctors of theology and doctors of the decretals with other eminent scholars, all skilled in the administration of justice. [He is determined] to conduct this trial in due and fitting form for the exaltation of the Faith and for the benefit of those who have been deceived and betrayed by this woman.

Item. And finally should those mentioned above or even one of them be unwilling to accept and to consent in obedience to what is herein stated, in the terms of this document, namely that although the capture of this woman is in no way equivalent to the capture of a king or prince or an individual of noble lineage, any one of whom, had he been captured, king or dauphin or other royal prince, the King of England, if he so willed, could have got possession of by giving the one who made the capture 10 thousand *livres,* according to the law, the practice, and the custom of France, therefore the Bishop, in the name of the King of England and in his own name demands and orders the above-mentioned to hand over the Maid to him for he guarantees the payment of 10 thousand *livres* in fulfillment of all conditions. As the law requires and under pain of its penalty the Bishop commands that the Maid be given up and handed over to him.

⚜ ⚜ ⚜

The letter from the University of Paris to John of Luxembourg, which I have mentioned already, is as follows: A TRUE COPY OF THE LETTER OF THE UNIVERSITY OF PARIS TO JOHN OF LUXEMBOURG FOR THE DELIVERANCE OF THE MAID

Most Illustrious, Respected, And Mighty Seigneur, We Commend Ourselves With Great Attachment To Your High Nobleness.

In your wondrous wisdom you know and acknowledge that all good Catholic Knights must, in the first place, devote themselves might and main to the service of God. The foremost solemn oath of the Order of Chivalry is, "To safeguard and uphold the honor of God, His Holy Church, and the Catholic Faith." Your memory of this oath served you well when the woman who calls herself *The Maid* was captured in the presence of your noble person and authority. Through her the honor of God is foully sullied, our Faith grievously wounded, and the Church too much discredited. She has occasioned the diffusion of idolatries, vain beliefs, evil doctrines, and other irreparable disorders and depravities in this kingdom. Verily, all Christians owe you a supreme debt of gratitude for your fruitful devotion to our Holy Faith and to this entire realm.

As for us we give thanks to God with all our hearts for your great valor and noble courage. A capture of such [importance] will become merely a little thing unless it brings about whatever is required to make amends for the offenses perpetrated by this woman against our very gentle Creator, His Faith, and His Holy Church. Her other misdeeds are innumerable.

It will be the greatest evil that ever was, an atrocious offense against Divine Majesty, if this affair languishes. She could be rescued, lost to us! It is rumored that certain of our foes are designing such a scheme, applying to their intention by means the most crafty, all their wiles. And, what is worse, by sums of money and threats of violence (*randon*).

Let us hope God will not allow a mischance so mischievous to afflict His people. May your illustrious good sense not tolerate it, but lead you to take steps to meet this emergency resolutely. If in any way her deliverance is brought about without condign atonement, what an irreparable disgrace for your high nobleness and for all others who may meddle in this affair. Let a stop be put at once even to the possibility of such a shocking deed. This is imperative! Therefore, because delay involves too serious a risk, one very injurious to the realm, we, with genuine humility and devoted attachment, pray your honored and puissant nobleness to give up this woman and have her brought to justice for the good and the grandeur of this kingdom, for the preservation of the Faith, and in the interest of Divine Honor. Send her without delay to the Inquisitor of the Faith who has required and does require her [to be delivered to him]. His purpose is to examine the merits of the grave accusation [against her], so that the will of God may be done and the people enlightened by the truth of sacred teaching, as is their due. Or if you prefer and choose, give up and deliver this woman to the Reverend Father in God, the highly honored Bishop of Beauvais, for as is well known she was made captive [in territory] under his jurisdiction. The Bishop and the Inquisitor are to be her judges in this Trial of Faith. Every Christian of whatever degree is bound [in conscience] to obey them, under solemn penalties of the law. By complying with this command you will gain the grace and the love of the Supreme Divinity and you will be an instrument for the exaltation of our Holy Faith. You will enhance the glory of your great and noble name and in an equal manner that of the most high and all powerful prince, the ever redoubtable Duke of Burgundy.

We then who are in your debt will beg God to bestow good fortune on your noble self. May He, Our Savior, direct you with Divine Grace in all your activities in this world and grant you happiness without limit in heaven.

Written in Paris, the 14th day of July 1430.

10

JOAN'S TRANSFER TO ROUEN

After the before-mentioned Summons and Letter were written and sent off, the Bishop of Beauvais, whose name was Peter Cauchon, set out from Paris with a representative of the University of Paris and an apostolic notary. They came to Compiègne where the Duke of Burgundy and John of Luxembourg were directing the siege before that city. To the Duke the Bishop showed the document with the Summons [to hand over the Maid]. After accepting this the Duke handed it to his Chancellor, Nicolas Rolin,

who was with him and said, "Give this to my Lord of
Beaurevoir, John of Luxembourg." In a little while the
Summons was presented to Luxembourg who accepted it
and read it. Then he was given the Letter of the University,
which he also read.

❧ ❧ ❧

In the affidavit of the apostolic notary, whose name was
Triquelot, mention is made only of the document of the
Summons. I append here my translation of his affidavit
from the original Latin.

In this year of grace one thousand four hundred and thirty, on
the sixteenth day of July, in the thirteenth year of the pontifi-
cate of Pope Martin V, in the headquarters of the very renowned prince, the Duke of Burgundy, set up before the
besieged city of Compiègne, and in the presence of the distinguished knights, Nicolas of Mailly, the bailiff of Vermandois,
and John of Pressy, with a large number of eminent individuals,
etc., the Reverend Father in God, Peter, Bishop and Count of
Beauvais, handed to the very illustrious prince, the Duke
of Burgundy, a Summons written on paper containing the five
articles, word for word, as you may read in the true copy of
this document inserted above. This Summons the duke (I
report this truthfully) gave to his honorable servitor, Nicolas
Rolin, his Chancellor who was present. The duke ordered him
in turn to give it to the noble and powerful lord, John of Luxembourg, the Lord of Beaurevoir. The Chancellor gave this
Summons to John of Luxembourg who thus received it, as I
in truth saw. These facts that I write here took place in my
presence.

Signed, TRIQUELOT,
Apostolic and Royal Notary and Copyist.

❧ ❧ ❧

When the Summons with the Letter of the University
were presented and taken, as I have said, the Bishop spoke

with the Duke of Burgundy and John of Luxembourg. After a number of explanations a satisfactory agreement was reached. For a specified sum of money offered by the Bishop, the Maid would be handed over to him. Three or four days later this was done. The Bishop took the Maid and then gave her over to the English in whose hands she was brought to Rouen, where, thrown into the strong prison of the castle in that city, she was well jailed, well shackled, and well guarded.

✤ ✤ ✤

Here I must add a pertinent letter of the King of England. A TRUE COPY OF THE LETTER OF THE KING OF ENGLAND RELATING TO JOAN THE MAID AND THE BISHOP OF BEAUVAIS

Henry By The Grace Of God King Of England, To All Those To Whom These Presents May Come, Greeting

For some time past it has been known to all and it is notorious that a woman who insisted on being called *Joan the Maid,* discarding the garb and vesture of the female sex, an act repugnant and forbidden by all law, a deed contrary to Divine Law and abhorrent to God, put on and wore men's garments and likewise armed herself as a man.

She has perpetrated and been the occasion of ruthless homicides. And as it is established, she let it be noised about among simple folk, to lead them astray and deceive them, that she was sent by God and knew His divine secrets. This is not all. She made many other dogmatic assertions, all very perilous, all the occasion of prejudice and scandal to our Catholic Faith.

While occupied with these abominations, continued with hostility in opposition to Us and Our subjects, she, in her armor, was taken prisoner at Compiègne by one of Our faithful subjects. Since then under guard she has been brought to us [in Rouen]. And because of superstitions, erroneous doctrines, and other crimes of lese majeste against the Divinity, as is well known she was suspected repeatedly and reputed as notorious and defamed and under suspicion. In consequence We have been petitioned earnestly and insistently by the Reverend Father in God, Our loved and loyal counsellor, the Bishop of Beauvais, who is, for this Joan, the Ordinary and the Ecclesiastical Judge of the Church. She was apprehended and captured within the borders and boundaries of his diocese. In exactly the same way we have been exhorted by Our very dear and well-beloved daughter, the University of Paris, to be willing to allow this Joan to be given over, yielded up, and delivered to the said Reverend Father in God to interrogate and examine the said Joan on these crimes mentioned above and further to take legal action against her in accordance with the statutes and canons of the laws of God and the Church, and finally, to summon those who shall be made to come to the Bishop.

Therefore, WE, for the reverence and honor of the name of God, for the defense and exaltation of Holy Church and the Catholic Faith, yearn with devotion to accede, as a true and humble child of Holy Church, to the entreaties and exhortations of the said Reverend Father in God and the appeals of the Doctors and Masters of the said University of Paris, Our daughter. WE charge and command that at all times and whenever it shall be deemed necessary by the Reverend Father in God, this Joan shall be brought and transferred to him, actually and in fact, by Our officials and soldiers who guard her, so that he may interrogate and examine her and conduct her trial in accordance with [the will] of God, with what is right, and with the laws of God and the Church.

Therefore, WE issue a mandate to Our said officials and soldiers who have this Joan under guard that they bring and transfer her to the said Reverend Father in God, actually and in fact, without the least refusal or objections each and every time that they shall be requested by him.

WE enjoin all our justices, officials, and subjects, whether French or English, not to put any obstacle or difficulty, actually and in fact, in the way of the said Reverend Father in God or in the way of all others who have been and will be summoned to attend, to be occupied with, and to pass judgment in the said trial. Let all those who will be solicited by the said Reverend Father in God give him aid, help, support, protection, and encouragement, under pain of severe punishment.

WE intend, if need be, to get this Joan back again and to have her again [in our power] if it should happen that she is not condemned and convicted of the crimes herein mentioned, in particular the specific ones and some others that touch and corrupt our Faith.

In testimony of this WE have had Our ordinary seal affixed in the absence of the great seal.

Given in Rouen the 3rd day of January, in the year of grace 1431, and of Our reign the 9th.

Thus signed: By the King at the relation of His Great Council

John de Rinel

❧ ❧ ❧

Within a determined short time the Bishop of Beauvais, at the solicitation of the King of England and the members of his Council, who desired the death of the Maid, betook himself to Rouen. To this city he summoned all the very renowned dignitaries, the most learned and lettered advocates and lawyers. Their names are written in the record of this trial. To those assembled the Bishop addressed these words,

I say and declare to you that your sovereign lord, the King of France and England, has been urged by the nobles and by the individuals of His Council, and by the University of Paris to proceed with the trial of a woman whose name is Joan, but who in vulgar language is called *the Maid*. She is accused of heresy, of black magic, as well as several other crimes and misdeeds.

Now as you know this woman was captured and taken prisoner in my diocese. Therefore it is up to me to conduct her trial. With your consent, I intend to apply myself to this task. I ask you to assist me in this charge so that I may make no mistake in these proceedings.

All those present gave answer: "We are prepared to obey the King. We will assist you readily during this trial."

Because at that time the archiepiscopal see had no incumbent, which meant that *jurisdiction* rested in the hands of the Chapter of the Church of Rouen, the Bishop Peter Cauchon found his way into the Chapter and repeated to the Dean and the Canons words of the same purport he had expressed the day before.

"Because I am not in my own diocese," he explained, "I beg you to give me permission and grant me the freedom to proceed [with this trial] in the territory of the Archbishop of Rouen. Allow me to work here." He was accorded this privilege. Then he concluded, "May I have your agreement in writing?" This too was approved.

II

JOAN CONDEMNED

Protests were made to the Bishop that Joan the Maid had the right to be transferred to the [church] prison of the Archbishop of Rouen, because her trial in an ecclesiastical court was on a problem of faith [the crime of heresy]. However, in spite of these protests the good Bishop *(le bon seigneur)*, ever disdainful, preferred to satisfy the King of England and court the favor of the English by leaving her in the prison of these Englishmen, her mortal enemies. In this way he commenced to reveal his deliberate determination to administer "righteous justice."

During this trial he and his adherents showed themselves no less determined on the death of the Maid than Caiphas, Annas, and the scribes and pharisees were for the death of Our Saviour. This is clear, in plain view, in the transcript of the trial. In two copies I came across several lies. Conflicting differences are in what is written there, particularly in the [report of] her replies to some questions. In Joan's trial of vindication it is rightly proved that the [transcript] of her trial of condemnation was altered fraudulently in several instances.

❧ ❧ ❧

JOAN'S LAST DAY ON EARTH

In The Year Of Our Lord 1431, This Wednesday, Next To The Last Day Of May, Was The Last Day Of The Trial.

The Legal Citation

Summoned by our authority to appear in person and to listen to the decision [of the court] in our presence, Joan [was] in the Old Market Place of the city of Rouen at eight in the morning to hear herself proclaimed, "A Relapsed Heretic, Excommunicated," with the usual announcements made on such occasions.

Later on in the morning of that day, toward nine o'clock, We, the Bishop, Peter Cauchon, and the Judges for the trial, were in the Old Market Place close to the church of St. Savior. Present and in attendance were the Bishop of Thérouanne and the Bishop of Noyon with a number of doctors, clerics, and lawyers. At the conclusion of the sermon preached to Joan, we admonished her for the salvation of her soul to resolve to be penitent for her wicked deeds. That she might be truly contrite we designated two friars of the Order of Preachers to be there near her for the sole purpose of giving her continual spiritual guidance.

After these endeavors just mentioned We, the Bishop, and the Deputy of the Inquisitor [were] mindful of the details above, in which it is manifest that Joan, by persistence in her wickedness, had feigned sorrow and contrition with evil intent and diabolic obstinacy. She had profaned the divine and holy name of God, an act of damnable blasphemy. By proving herself an irreclaimable heretic, relapsed and in error, she is worthless and not in the least deserving of any mercy.

THEREFORE, we pronounce this Final Sentence:

IN THE NAME OF THE LORD, AMEN

WE, Peter Cauchon, by divine mercy, the lowly Bishop of Beauvais, and Friar John Le Maître, the Deputy of the Inquisitor of the Faith, judges competent in this action,

WHEREAS, we deem you, Joan, who call yourself the Maid, to be a relapsed heretic, fallen into a diversity of crimes and offenses, schism, idolatry, invocation of demons, and sundry other evils, and

WHEREAS, in our just judgment we have so declared you,

However, because the Church never folds its arms against those who have the will to come back to her,

WE were of the opinion that, after full deliberation and in full good faith you had turned away from all the evils you had cast off, when you promised, vowed, and swore publicly never to embrace them again, nor any other heresies whatsoever, but, instead, to abide in union and communion with the Catholic Church and with our Holy Father the Pope, exactly as this is embodied in the abjuration to which you set your own hand,

Nevertheless, and this we cry out with deep grief, "You are for the second time a relapsed heretic, like a dog which has the habit of going back to its vomit!" Therefore, we proclaim, "You have reincurred the sentence of excommunication under which you first fell. You have fallen back into your former sins. WE PRONOUNCE YOU A HERETIC."

From our tribunal in this court of justice, by this sentence in these written terms, be it known,

WE throw you out of the unity of the Church, we discard you as a rotten member.

WE give you up to secular justice, which we beg to deal with you gently and generously in relation to your life and your person.

Joan Put to Death

When this judgment was heard, the bishop, the inquisitor, and a number of the judges betook themselves away from this place and allowed Joan to remain on the scaffold alone.

At once the bailiff of Rouen, an Englishman, who was ready, without further formality, without even pronouncing any sentence of death against her, ordered Joan taken to the space for her burning.

Joan, listening to this command, wept and cried out in bewilderment, so that she moved the people and all those present to tears of compassion.

Without the least delay the bailiff ordered the fire lit. This was done.

And there she was burned shockingly, martyred indeed, an example of monstrous cruelty.

For this reason a number of persons, some individuals of importance, others just plain people, muttered wrathfully against the English.

EPILOGUE

The Aftermath—Letters of Agitated and Fulsome Explanation

A TRUE COPY OF THE LETTER OUR KING [HENRY VI] WROTE TO THE PRELATES OF THE CHURCH, TO THE DUKES AND COUNTS AND OTHER NOBLES, AND TO THE LOYAL CITIES OF OUR REALM IN FRANCE

Reverend Father in God,
It is sufficiently well-known, reports are scattered in every direction, that a woman who had herself called *Joan the*

Maid, an erring prophetess dressed like a man these two years or more, a state of affairs contrary to divine law and to the condition of the female sex, an abomination to God, while arrayed in this fashion was brought to our foremost enemy [Charles VII]. To him and his adherents—churchmen, nobles, and the people—she gave to understand (and she did this often) that she was sent by God. She prided herself presumptuously on frequent and private messages from St. Michael in person, as well as from a great multitude of heavenly angels and saints, for instance, St. Catherine and St. Margaret. Through such deceits and by the guarantee of assured future victories she beguiled and deluded many.

She diverted the minds of men and women from the way of truth. She led them to a belief in fables and falsehoods. This is not all. She put on armor like a Knight or Equerry and designed a banner and what is more outrageous, through excessive pride and presumption she made the demand to have and to display the truly noble and surpassing Royal Arms of France. For this she was granted only partial permission. But she did display them during several battles and sieges, she and her brothers too, as is well-known, namely, a shield azure, with two golden fleurs-de-lys and a sword point upward with its tip encircled by a crown! In such manner she took the field to lead groups and even whole companies of men-at-arms and archers. She caused and inflicted inhuman cruelties by shedding blood, by fomenting disorder and sedition, by cajoling the people to perjury and pernicious revolt, and to superstition and false beliefs. She disrupted all possibility of real peace by reviving a languishing war.

She allowed people to venerate and worship her as a saintly woman. She did damnable work in divers other ways, too long to relate here but well-known in certain localities.

Nearly the whole of Christianity has been scandalized by such actions.

II

God in his Power took pity on His loyal people. He did not leave them long in peril nor did He suffer them to abide in the new credulity, vain and perilous as it was, into which they had entered without heed. In His great mercy and forbearance He permitted this woman to be captured at Compiègne and to be placed under our authority and control. Since then the Bishop of the diocese in which she was taken, in his office as her ecclesiastical judge, has claimed her as a notorious woman of evil reputation, guilty of the crime of lese majeste against God.

WE, both out of respect for our Holy Mother the Church, whose saintly decrees we prefer to our own personal desires and will, and for this further reason, the honor and exaltation of our Holy Faith, ordered the above-mentioned Joan consigned to the Bishop so that he might bring her to justice. WE did not wish the lawyers and officials who administer justice in our civil courts to concern themselves with the punishment and penalty in her case (insofar as this is justifiable and within our legal rights) after WE weighed the heavy damages, the troubles, the horrible killings, the detestable cruelties, and other innumerable evils she had committed against our realm and our loyal, obedient subjects.

The Bishop in association with the Deputy Inquisitor for Heresy and Error opened the trial of this woman Joan with great solemnity and all due formality in the presence of a distinguished number of skilled professors, doctors of theology, and doctors of canon law. The Bishop and the Inquisitor, her judges in these legal proceedings, had this woman Joan interrogated on diverse occasions for several days. Her assertions and admissions were examined exhaustively by the said professors and doctors, and then broadly speaking, by all the Faculties of our dear and well-beloved daughter, the University of Paris, to whom the said assertions and admissions were sent.

In conformity with the decision and pronouncement [of the University] the Judges found Joan guilty on charges of superstition, prophecy, and idolatry, a woman who had invoked devils and blasphemed God and His saints, a schismatic gone far astray from the Faith of Jesus Christ. To convert her, to bring her back to Holy Mother the Church, to cleanse her of such horrible, detestable, and pernicious sins and crimes, to heal her soul and save it from eternal damnation, she was often and at great length very gently and very charitably admonished that with all her errors cast away and left behind she could return humbly to the straight path and the way of truth, otherwise she put herself in grave peril of soul and body.

III

Alas, as already noted, that very dangerous spirit of pride and outrageous presumption, which strives without ceasing to perturb and prevent the union and safety of faithful Christians, so held her mind and filled her heart that Joan, obstinate and hardened against every sane doctrine, sound counsel, and tender exhortation, refused to soften her heart and humble herself. On the contrary she boasted frequently that everything she did was done well, that all she undertook was by command of God and the saintly virgins who appeared to her visibly. What is worse, she said she recognized and would recognize on this earth only [the authority] of God alone and that of *her* saints of heaven. She refused and rejected the authority of our Holy Father the Pope, that of a general council and of the Universal Church

Militant. Her ecclesiastical judges, realizing during the long period of time [of her trial] her hardened and obstinate spirit, had her brought before the clergy and the people gathered in great numbers. In their presence a renowned doctor of theology presented a review of her case in a sermon in which he publicly and solemnly explained and exposed her crimes and errors, for the exaltation of our Christian faith, the up-rooting of errors, the edification and improvement of Christian people. She was charitably admonished anew to return to the unity of Holy Church and to correct her failings and her errors. Even after this she remained obstinate and opinionated.

IV

For this reason the judges, in accordance with the law and established practice in such a case, proceeded to pronounce sentence against her. But before this sentence was read in its entirety, she made a move, or so it seemed, to discard her stubborn spirit, announcing she wished to return to Holy Church. Her judges and the clergy heard this with joy and right good will, hoping in this way to retrieve her soul and body from torment and perdition. Then she submitted herself to the authority of the Church. She revoked and abjured publicly, with words from her own lips, her errors and her detestable crimes. She signed with her own hand the document of revocation and abjuration. Then our Holy Mother Church who rejoices over the one sinner who does penance, desiring to bring back to the fold the sheep strayed and lost in the desert, condemned this woman Joan to prison [for life] to do salutary penance. She had barely returned to prison before the fire of her pride, which had seemed extinct, was ablaze with flames fanned by the pestilential breath of the Devil. Before long this wretched woman fell back into the fatuous follies and errors she had previously held, the ones, as I have explained, she did abjure and revoke. Therefore, in conformity with the decrees and edicts of Holy Mother the Church, this woman, fallen again, indeed, into her former errors and blasphemies, was given over to civil justice and straightway condemned to be burned in the fire, lest she hereafter contaminate other followers of Our Lord Jesus Christ. Realizing the approach of death she fully admitted and confessed that the spirits she said had appeared to her so often were evil ones and liars. She admitted that their promise of her deliverance was a deceit. She confessed that these spirits had mocked and betrayed her.

The case is closed! This woman and her work ended in death!

V

WE notify you now, Reverend Father in God, to acquaint you with the whole truth of this affair, so that wherever you may deem it appropriate in your diocese, sermons may be delivered in public or in another manner to proclaim these facts for the benefit and advantage of our Holy Faith and for the edification of Christian people, wronged and deceived for so long a time by the mischief of this woman and her work. By these means you will provide yourself with the power, as it behooves your eminent authority, to save every individual soul confided to your care from audacious, heedless faith in such errors and perilous superstitions. One noticeable peculiarity of the present age is the appearance of several false prophets and sowers of damnable errors and false beliefs who with foolhardy daring and outrageous presumption rise up against our Holy Mother the Church. They would, perforce, pollute Christianity with the poison of false belief, unless Christ Our Lord in His Mercy forestall them and unless you and His other officials, as behooves you, work together with perseverance to punish and destroy the whims and the perfidious daring of these reprobates.

GIVEN IN OUR CITY OF ROUEN THE 28TH DAY OF JUNE 1431.

[This next letter of Henry VI was written to guarantee royal protection for everyone in any way concerned with the trial of Joan of Arc.]

A TRUE COPY OF THE LETTER OF HENRY VI, DATED 12 JUNE 1431

Henry By The Grace Of God, King Of France And England, To All Those To Whom These Presents May Come, Greeting

It is now some time since WE heeded the pleas and the petition of our very dear and truly well-beloved daughter, the University of Paris, that a woman who had herself called *Joan the Maid* and who was captured while bearing arms by one of our subjects in the diocese of Beauvais within the limits of the spiritual jurisdiction of the bishop of that see, be given up, handed over, and transferred to the Church. She was a notorious woman, unfavorably known and under suspicion of having said, repeated, and spread in several and varied places and regions of our Realm of France distinctly dangerous errors. To the great scandal of the entire Christian world she committed, perpetrated, and was guilty of excesses, misdeeds, and crimes most monstrous against our Holy Catholic Faith. On several and different occasions WE were requested and urged with diligent insistence by our beloved and faithful counsellor, the Bishop of Beauvais, the judge in ordinary of this woman, to consent to surrender, transfer, and deliver her to him, to judge, punish, and sentence her—provided that, after a trial conducted in due and lawful form, she was found guilty and convicted of the above-mentioned errors, crimes, excesses, and offenses, or anyone or several of them.

WE as a good Catholic and son of the Church, following in the footsteps of our predecessors, the Kings of France and England, did not wish to do anything that could or might, in any way, delay or obstruct the Holy Inquisition of our Hallowed Faith. With the realization that the proceedings of the Holy Inquisition are preferable to those of secular and temporal justice in rendering to every individual what is his by right, [WE] gave an order to have this woman transferred and delivered to our Counsellor, her judge in ordinary as indicated above, for him to inquire into her errors, crimes, excesses, and offenses and to institute legal proceedings against her insofar as he deemed this justified. For these proceedings the Deputy Inquisitor, in the absence of the Inquisitor, was associated with the Bishop, our Counsellor. Together they conducted their investigation and the trial against this woman's errors, crimes, excesses, and offenses so well that in their final sentence this woman, after she had positively and in public abjured her errors, crimes, excesses, and offenses, embraced them again (this is clear in the record of her trial), and, at last, was declared a relapsed heretic, cast aside, abandoned, and handed over to the secular court in which she was condemned to be burned and to die in the fire. In this way she was put to death.

II

Should there perchance be some who give the errors and misdeeds of this woman their approval or others who decide and endeavor perversely, through hatred or vengeance or other motives, to interfere with the lawful judgment of our Holy Mother the Church and to draw from the legal action of those responsible for the trial [of this woman] cause to cite before our Holy Father or the General Council or any other court of law the Reverend Father in God, the

Bishop of Beauvais, the Deputy of the Inquisitor, the Doctors, the Masters, the Clergy, the Plaintiffs, the Lawyers, the Counsellors, the Notaries, or any others active in this trial,

WE, as the Protector and Defender of our Holy Catholic Faith are resolved to support, sustain, and defend the said Judges, Doctors, Masters, Clergy, Plaintiffs, Lawyers, Counsellors, Notaries, and all others who were active in any manner whatever during this particular trial, and to support, sustain, and defend them in all they declared and decided in each and every detail of the circumstances and conditions that surround and affect this trial, so that from this time forth all Judges, Doctors, Masters, and all others [concerned] shall be more inclined, disposed, and encouraged to promote and undertake, without fear or dismay, the extirpation of errors and false doctrines which—and we say this with sorrow—arise and multiply in this present time through various regions of Christianity.

WE have been duly and personally informed that the said trial began and ended with the deliberation, the justice, and the reverence required by the laws of the Church. For this and the further reason that the burden of the accusation [against this woman] was based upon the decisions of the Doctors and Masters of the Faculties of Theology and of Decrees of the University of Paris, our very dear and well-beloved daughter, and upon the opinions of a group of Bishops, Abbots, and Prelates, all Doctors, Masters, and Clerks, expert in the laws of God and the Church, with other churchmen in great numbers, of whom the entire group or the greater part were daily present and in attendance with the said Judges, questioning this woman and conducting her trial,

WE pledge our word as King to aid and defend and to give aid and defense at our personal cost and expense, in court and out of court, if it happen that any individual whatever (regardless of his state, dignity, degree, preeminence and authority, be he Judge, Doctor, Master, Clerk, Plaintiff, Lawyer, Counsellor, Notary, or anyone else) who was concerned with, worked for or was heard during the trial [of this woman] should be summoned to appear on account of this trial and its circumstances, before our Holy Father the Pope, or the General Council, or before the Commissioners or Deputies of either, or in any other way.

On their behalf in such a court action, WE for the honor of God, respect for the Church, and the defense of our Holy Faith, will oppose the legal proceedings brought against any of these persons, no matter what their state or circumstances, and WE will pursue this course under every aspect and point of law and legality, at our own expense.

III

WE command all our Ambassadors and Messengers, those of the Blood Royal and Lineage and all others, who are or will be in the Court of Rome or at the General Council, all Bishops, Prelates, Doctors, and Masters, all our subjects and loyal followers in our realms of France and England, and the Procurators of our Kingdoms in the Court of Rome, and each of them, in every instance when they hear or have cognizance (or there be need as the occasion abovementioned arises) that the Judges, Doctors, Masters, Clerks, Plaintiffs, Lawyers, Counsellors, Notaries, and others or any one of them, are to be brought to court and tried before the Pope, the Council, or other legal authority, to join together in our name, without the least delay, for the aid and defense of the above-mentioned Judges, Doctors, Masters, Clerks, Plaintiffs, Lawyers, Counsellors, Notaries, and all others or any one of them by all ways and means, canonical and juridical. Let them require the subjects of our Realms, present here at this time, and the subjects of the Kings, Princes, and Nobles, allied and in league with us to give them aid, counsel, favor, and assistance in this matter by all possible ways and means without the least delay or difficulty.

In witness whereof we have had our ordinary seal affixed to these presents in the absence of the great seal.

Dated at Rouen, the 12th day of June in the year of grace 1431 and of our reign the 9th.

[On the fold]
By the King at the relation of his Great Council. Present were the Cardinal of England [Henry Beaufort], You [the Chancellor of France, Louis of Luxembourg], the Bishop of Beauvais [Peter Cauchon], the Bishop of Noyon [Jean de Mailly], and the Bishop of Norwich [William Alnwick], with the Earl of Warwick [Richard Beauchamp], and the Earl of Stafford [Humphrey Buckingham], the Abbot of Fécamp [Gilles de Duremont], and the Abbot of Mont St. Michel [Robert Jolivet], and [John] Lord Stafford, [Ralph] Lord Cromwell, [John] Lord Tiptoft, Peter Count of St. Pol, and several others.

Thus signed: CALOT

COMMENTS ON THE LIFE OF JOAN OF ARC

PROLOGUE
(p 13 to p 14)

With his remark, "The chronicles differ and disagree," the compiler of this first *Life* awakens interesting expectations. He increases our interest when he lists the chronicles he has read: Froissart, Monstrelet, Gaguin. Although he does not say directly that his intention is to point out his sources (this is a battered word but there is none to take its place) his purpose is to make a favorable impression on his readers by telling them where he has searched for his details. With an air of disarming frankness he seems to list his "recognized authorities."

Jean Froissart (1338-1410?) of course, he knew he must mention to give his readers a definite assurance of the breadth of his own reading. He knew better than we may understand now that no one of his day expected him to find a word about Joan of Arc in Froissart. Yet the very purpose or reason for his writing about Joan of Arc at all was based upon the systematic design Froissart followed; his philosophy of history was to point out events of the recent past in France and England "worthy of lasting memory."

Here is Froissart's explanation of his appreciation of the value of history taken from page 1 of volume 1 in Thomas Johne's translation of the *Chronicles of England and France*. . . . We use the 1839 edition.

That the honourable enterprises, noble adventures, and deeds of arms performed in the wars between England and France may be properly related and held *in perpetual remembrance*—to the end that brave men taking example from them may be encouraged in their well-doing, I sit down to record a history deserving great praise. . . .

Monstrelet (1400-1453) is another matter. It is gratifying to have him mentioned by the compiler without the slightest antipathy to his fervent Anglo-Burgundian judgment on Joan of Arc. (Our indication of chapters in Monstrelet refers to Buchon's edition.) In chapter LIX of Bk. 2 Monstrelet depicts the feelings of the inhabitants of Orléans during the oppressive siege before the coming of Joan of Arc. They are, he says, aware of the peril of falling "into the servitude and subjection of their enemies [the English]." (*En la servitude et obéyssance de leurs ennemis.*) Our compiler writes of the thanks the French owe to God for freeing them from that fall "into the servitude and subjection of their old enemies, the English." (*En la subiection et servitude des anciens ennemys de France, les Angloys.*) Monstrelet has been of service.

Now and in what measure *Robert Gaguin* was used will be pointed out later on. He was a friend of Erasmus and he wrote a history, not a compiled chronicle. The "Great Chronicles of France" are better known as the *Great Chronicles of Saint Denis*. After the death of Charles VI on 21 October 1422 these records were not continued until Jean Chartier took up the task in 1437. The compiler owes Chartier's *Chronicle of Charles VII* an enormous debt. Our references are to Vallet de Viriville's edition. The so-called *Journal d'un Bourgeois de Paris* is a source the compiler for his own reasons preferred not to mention. The sentence, "[Joan was] burned to death in the city of Rouen for her misdeeds," is a direct quotation. (*Journal*, Tuétey's ed., p. 354).

When the compiler wrote, "All the work she did was by command of God," he took this from Joan's words during the trial. On Wednesday 2 May she told her judges, "In regard to my work and my words, as I have explained before, I refer and submit them all to God, who ordered me to do what I have done."

1. THE ENGLISH LAY SIEGE TO ORLÉANS
(p 14 to p 16)

This section's first paragraph does not squander details in its succinct summary of eleven terrible years of invasion. From 1 August 1417, when Henry V relanded in France to recover "the old dominion of Aquitaine and the duchy of Normandy" (Burne, *The Agincourt War,* 115), to the first day in the siege of Orléans, 12 October 1428, the ignoble art of war created disaster for both England and France. The folios of the chronicles, French, Burgundian, and English, overflow with heroism and horror, futile death and noble devotion, as they record that tumultuous era when "Normandy, Picardy, Champagne, Maine, Anjou, Touraine, and Beauce" felt the logical results of fifteenth-century politics gone awry, the flail of war.

When our compiler dates the beginning of the siege *1429,* he is copying from Jean Chartier, who, in his chapter 32 wrote, "L'an mil CCCC vingt et neuf fust mis le siege devant la ville d'Orleans par le conte de Salbery." (Vallet de Viriville's edition I, 60). Chartier is not the source of the remark reducing the number of forts built by the English around Orléans to four. We have not discovered where this falsely precise information came from.

In his design to keep his paragraphs sparse the compiler discards any discussion of the two plans the English had "for their advance" south into France. This problem proposed a choice, Orléans or Angers. Bedford argued for Angers. He lost and never went near Orléans. How this came about is submerged in the rigid silence of official records. Had his scheme developed into an actual attack on the city in Anjou, Joan of Arc would be known as "The Maid of Angers," a destructive blow to that strange segment of French opinion which, by using the phrase "Maid of Orléans" as a pretext, claims to believe Joan was the bastard daughter of the Duke of Orléans and Isabelle of Bavaria, Charles VI's queen. The Estates of Normandy, meeting in Rouen, that is, the authorized representatives of the higher clergy, the nobility, and the wealthy merchants, were told in July 1428 by Pierre Surreau, who was charged with receiving and disbursing English government funds in France, and who had attended the deliberations of the Great Council in Paris, that Orléans not Angers was to be besieged. (Bibl. Nat., MS fr. 4488, folios 655-56).

☙ ☙ ☙

Bedford had valid political reasons not to approve of Joan of Arc. She was a mere girl who crumbled the English dream of conquest. He penned his bitter opinion of the girl and of the choice of Orléans over Angers in a furious letter of 1433 written to Henry VI: "And all things in [France] prospered for you till the time of the siege of Orléans, *taken in hand, God knoweth by what advice.* At the which time . . . there fell, by the hand of God, as it seemed, a great stroke upon your people . . . caused in great part . . . [by] a disciple and limb of the Fiend, called the Pucelle, that used false enchantments and sorcery." (Proceedings and Ordinances of the Privy Council of England, IV, 223).

Today England harbors two opposed estimates of Joan of Arc. One is favorable, the other echoes Bedford. A pungent example of this was penned in 1961 by the brilliant critic and novelist, Rayner Heppenstall, for whom Joan remains "That dreadful girl, the most detrimental figure in European history." (*The Fourfold Tradition,* 33).

☙ ☙ ☙

The geographical litany of the regions of France "seized and held" by the English—"Normandy, Picardy, Champagne, Maine, Anjou, Touraine, and Beauce" (this last the portion of Orléanais north of the Loire) is, with the exception of Touraine, satisfactory. Thomas Duke of Clarence had penetrated into Anjou as far south as Baugé to die there in a brief, explosive military disaster. Salisbury then executed a brilliant retreat into Normandy, collected fresh troops, and thrust his return into Anjou with relentless vigor to reach the walls of Angers. But Anjou was never entirely in the hands of the English. Maine,

Domremy, an aerial view. Joan's home is in the center encircled by trees.

Domremy, the river Meuse and its valley in winter when Joan left home to begin her "work."

on the other hand, was captured completely. The shattering victory of Verneuil broke the barriers defending this region. Cruel defeats at Le Mans and Mayenne ended serious resistance there. For Champagne and Picardy the Duke of Burgundy held enough of both regions to make them secure for the English. Normandy, except for Mont St. Michel which never fell, endured an English yoke for decades. Touraine is the only misplaced item in the compiler's litany of losses. Fierbois, Loches, Chinon, Tours with the rest of Touraine were never wrenched from Charles VII. In each of these regions the temperature of sentiment favorable to Charles VII fluctuated. When it cooled into collaboration against him, the justification was the claim of an eternal French privilege, excessive individualism, sometimes a synonym for expediency. Pages of French history before Charles VII and after him up to the present are stamped with the claim of this disturbing distinction. The inflexible integrity of leaders as diverse as Joan of Arc and General de Gaulle represent, by contrast with this ever ripe opportunism, the real grandeur of France.

⚜ ⚜ ⚜

There is a remark in the manuscript that occasioned arguments with friends and acquaintances who pride themselves as being knowledgeable in French history or geography: "[The English] aimed at capturing [Orléans] to provide themselves with a passage . . . into the territory of Berry and Auvergne and other areas beyond . . . even as far as Lyons." Here Lyons was the stumbling block that bruised them the most. To assuage the pain of others who may be grazed by the mention of this city as an English objective at the time of Joan of Arc we offer the tranquilizing authority of this statement on p. 198 of Colonel Burne's study, *The Agincourt War*, ". . . towns as far distant as Lyons began to tremble for their safety." The opinion of Professor Jacob on page 191 of *The Fifteenth Century* should heal all afflicting doubts, ". . . at one time Salisbury looked likely to threaten Lyon."

These details—Salisbury's death, the direction of the siege, the embassy for Orléans to the Duke of Burgundy, and Bedford's reply of refusal—are taken from chapter 34 of Jean Chartier, pp. 63-66 in Vallet de Viriville's edition, and from Robert Gaguin's *Compendium super Francos*, Lib. X, folios CXVI to CXVII—the edition of 1504 in the Rare Book Collection of Yale University Library. Bedford's testy reply to Burgundy, after the emissaries from Orléans visited him, is put into a stimulating Latin rendering by Gaguin, folio CXVII, lines 5-7, "Audita legatione Bethfortus non ego, inquit, dumos sentesque discussi ut alter avibus potiatur. Aurelianenses pro mea voluntate subjugatos recipiam et quas per totam obsidionem impensas feci eas compessabunt."

2. JOAN OF ARC MEETS CHARLES VII
(p 17 to p 22)

The Voices: Details about this "young girl called Joan" are from Chartier, ch. 36, the *Geste des nobles,* ch. 250, the *Chron. de la Pucelle,* chs. 42-43, and the *Minutes* of her trial. Her reluctance to confide in her parents, glanced at in *Chron. de la Pucelle,* is argued in detail during the trial. She was asked on Thursday 22 February 1431, the second day she appeared before her judges, "What instruction did your Voices give you for the good of your soul?" Her reply explained, "My Voices said it was necessary for me to go into France but my father must know nothing about it." She added, "I went to an uncle's house. He brought me to Robert de Baudricourt."

Two weeks and three days later, on Monday 12 March, the prickly subject came up again. "Do you believe you did well to leave home without permission of your father and mother?" Joan retorted, "I obeyed them well in everything except about leaving home. But since then I wrote them a letter and they forgave me." And, *there are those who declare Joan could neither read nor write!*

The pious judges, not impressed, continued, "Did you ask your Voices if you should tell your father and mother of your going?" Joan explained patiently, "My Voices were willing enough for me to tell my father and mother—but they would have put difficulties in my way, if I had. For my part, nothing could have made me tell them! My Voices gave me this choice: tell your father and mother or say nothing." There is a curious variation here from her first explanation. The devout judges, not yet nagged into irritation by the length of the trial, let it pass. The magic of her voice, the mystery of her presence were still in her favor.

The author of the *Journal d'un Bourgeois de Paris* wrote in his diary for 1431, after Joan's death, "St. Catherine and St. Margaret appeared to her and said, 'Go to a captain whom we will name.' She went but without the permission of her father or mother." (ed. Tuétey, 267.) He was a University of Paris adherent, embarrassed as his Alma Mater was, by the Maid.

Ville Robert: Robert de Baudricourt did give Joan an escort for her hazardous, foolhardy, successful voyage to Chinon. "Ville Robert," mentioned only by Chartier, was not one of the group. We are almost convinced that Chartier's secretary, ever absent-minded, was thinking as he wrote of someone named Robert whose nickname was "ville," an Old French form of *veille*, and this would mean perhaps "Robert the Night Watch" (see Littré). Baudricourt's first name helped his inattention. Joan gave a summary account of her journey to the inquisitive judges. On Thursday 22 February 1431, this detail was in her remarks, "When I left Vaucouleurs I was accompanied by a knight, and esquire, and four servitors." We learn the names of her escort from witnesses for her vindication.

The Sword: The mysterious sword is another matter. During the trial on Tuesday, 27 February 1431, Joan answered the first questions of the subtle Doctor of Theology Jean Beaupère. Learned but cautious, he was wise, he thought, to seek a possible influence of sorcery in this sword. He began, "Did you ever go to St. Catherine de Fierbois?" Joan's detailed reply said in part,

71

Yes, and one day while I was there I heard three Masses. From St. Catherine de Fierbois I went on to Chinon . . . While I was in Tours —it may have been Chinon—I sent this request for a sword which was in the church of St. Catherine de Fierbois:

SEARCH OUT A SWORD WHICH IS IN THE CHURCH BEHIND THE ALTAR. It was found at once but was all covered with rust.

Beaupère broke in at this point to inquire, "How did you know the sword was there?" Joan kept on as if she had not heard. "The sword was in the ground. It was rusty and five crosses were marked on it." Then as if she caught his question,

I knew it was there because my Voices told me. I never saw the man who went to look for it. I had written to the priests of that place to ask them for the sword. They sent it. It seems to me it was a little underground behind the altar. However, I am not sure exactly if it was in front or behind the altar, but I think I wrote at the time that the sword was behind the altar. When it was located the clergy of the church rubbed it hard (*confricaverunt*) and all at once the rust dropped off without injury [to the sword]. It was an armorer (*armarius*) of Tours—some manuscripts call him "a dealer in weapons" (*mercator armorum*)—who went to search for it. The priests of St. Catherine presented me with a scabbard. At the same time the priests of Tours had two others made, one of deep red velvet, the second of golden cloth. I had another made of very tough leather.

We believe that the writer of this *Life* never read what Joan said about the sword at the trial. He relied exclusively on the chronicles at his disposal. This explains why he accepts their not-quite-correct details in the first place, the "five fleurs-de-lys" instead of Joan's "five crosses." He takes this peculiar error from Jean Chartier, the original and much-copied source of the confusion. Long ago in 1858 Vallet de Viriville examined all the extant manuscripts and printed copies of Chartier. A few mention "five little swords" but by far the greater number repeat "five fleurs-de-lys." Not a single one is satisfied with Joan's readily understood description. We think the good monk knew better. He preferred, we venture to say, a symbol of monarchy to one of religion. A less likely explanation has been suggested to us, namely, that the scribe, toiling away for Jean Chartier and reading the *Chron. de la Pucelle,* was captivated by the description there of the scabbard and transferred his delight in it to the sword (*Chron.* p. 277). "When the sword was brought to her she had a scabbard made for it spangled with fleurs-de-lys (*parsemé*)."

Once put into circulation this specific mention of the symbol of French royalty continued to be repeated. The monk Pierre Empis, always concise, eschews numbers but holds to the symbol: "a sword on which fleurs-de-lys were engraved" (*une épée sur laquelle des lis étaient sculptés*). Readers will find Empis easily in Ayroles 3, 481. A resounding contrast with Empis is given in the *Chron. de Philippe de Vigneulles,* "On both sides this sword was marked and covered with fleurs-de-lys" (ed. Charles Bruneau, 2, 199), and in Robert Gaguin's *Compendium* which describes the "antiquum ensem inter sacras oblationes utraque parte liliis insculptum." (Bk X, fol. CXVII). Joan's account of the five crosses is followed faithfully in the *Chron. de la Pucelle* (p. 277) and by the *Journal du Siège* in its entry for Thursday 17 February 1429. With gay Italian enthusiasm the *Chronicle* of Antonio Morosini raises the number of crosses to nine (*Morosini* 3, 109). Two others tell of the sword without decoration. First, Italian Guerneri Berni writes, "Questa Pulzella si fece dare una spada che era in una chiesa," (Q 4, 519). Second, *The Clerk of the City of La Rochelle* goes into full details about the recovery of the sword but omits all mention of its embellishment (*Revue historique,* 1877, 4, 338). The *Chron. de Lorraine* transfers the discovery of the sword to the Cathedral of Chartres. In this chronicle when Joan met the king she demanded, "Make sure that I have the sword which is in Notre Dame of Chartres." (Q 4, 332.)

Caxton, a contemporary of Joan of Arc, does not mention her sword. Other English chroniclers, for example Edward Hall and Holinshed, both sources of *Henry VI, Part I,* do not neglect the weapon. Hall, aghast that "wise men did believe" Joan, exclaims, "What should I speake how she had by revelacion a swerde, to her appoynted in the churche of saincte

Katheryn of Fierboys in Torayne where she never had been."
Holinshed paints in more details,

Then at the Dolphins sending by hir assignement, from saint Kath-
arins church of Fierbois in Touraine (where she never had beene
and knew not) in a secret place there among old iron, and appointed
she hir sword to be sought out and brought hir, that with five floure
delices was graven on both sides, wherewith she fought and did
manie slaughters by hir owne hands. (Bullough's *Sources of Shakespeare*, pp. 27 and 75).

In *Henry VI, Part I*, Joan is heard to say,

I am prepar'd: here is my keen-edg'd sword,
Deck'd with five flower-de-luces on each side;
The which at Touraine, in Saint Katharine's churchyard,
Out of a great deal of old iron I chose forth.
(Act I, sc. 2, 98-101.)

A representative of German medieval culture, Eberhard
Windecke, added in his chronicle a new story, albeit a bloody
one, to the legend of the sword. Joan, angered at the reappear-
ance of two camp followers (*zwei fahrende Töchter*) she had
ordered away from the army, "drew her sword and cut off the
head of one of them. The girl died." (Lefèvre-Pontalis, *Les
Sources allemandes*, 99).

In the *Commentaries* of Pius II, Joan dispels Charles VII's
doubts and misgivings about reaching Reims for his coronation
with this terse vaunt, "With an invisible sword I will clear
your way." (Q 4, 510). Joan of Arc's sword of Fierbois once
just a fact became a legend with variegated nuances until the
fancy of a Renaissance Pope fashioned it into a spectral blade.
Variety adds piquant zest to the annals of a former day.

Joan's positive "No" to the question, "Were you ever in
St. Catherine de Fierbois?" would be a problem if it could not
be unraveled easily. Chartier again is the culprit. In the *Chron.
de la Pucelle* he read, "Did you ever see the sword before?"
Joan's reply was "No." Chartier shifted this "No" from the
sword to the locality where it was found. Why? Was he
humoring his desire to add a tint of the miraculous to the palette

of the marvelous his brush was using to portray Joan? Jean Bouchet in his *Annales d'Aquitaine* (Ayroles 3, 294) and Philippe de Vigneulles repeat this inept morsel. Joan the saint, frank, healthy, and refreshing, needs none of this offensive fervor. In the *Journal du Siège* the "No" does not go astray.

⚜ ⚜ ⚜

Joan's Skill: Echoes of the exclamations of surprise and delight in Chinon over Joan's horsemanship and her skill with a lance (the type of lance she used is never specified) found an immediate response of admiration in the pens of Joan's contemporaries. A letter of 22 April 1429, written in Lyons and sent to Brussels, reports, "Each day the Maid in armor, astride a horse and with a lance in her hand rides with the king's forces." Edmond de Dynther's chronicle repeats this word for word (Ay. 3, 539; Q 4, 426). The monk who wrote the *first* mention of Joan put this information in his chronicle between 18 and 30 June 1429. "She performs wondrous deeds of arms. She handles the thrust of a lance with great power and readily avails herself of its aid, as can be seen day after day." The clerk who recorded news as it reached La Rochelle wrote in his register,

As soon as her armor was made she put it on, went out into the fields of Poitiers with other armed combatants where she handled her lance as well or better than any man there. She rode spirited chargers, the capricious ones that no one else dared mount without fear. (p. 338)

Poitiers is a slip of the pen but the admiration is correct.

These earliest reports take her strength for granted. Later writers, more satisfactory about her energy, are sometimes contradictory. In the *Chron. de la Pucelle* Joan is "strong with a well-formed body." The Augustinian friar, Jacobo Philippo Bergamo, whose remarkable imagination located Orléans on the Rhone, describes Joan as "small in stature indeed but very strong (*praevalida*) in her entire body." Alain Bouchard prefers her "tall and very beautiful." The *Chron. de Lorraine* says Joan was "a young girl of great vigor and strength, tall and powerful." Holinshed agrees: "Of favour was she counted likesome, of person stronglie made and manlie, of courage great, hardie, and stout withall. . . ."

In sworn testimony for her vindication in 1456 two of Joan's intimate friends recall her skill with horse and lance. She took a natural delight in her dazzling energy. Her audience did too. The Duke of Alençon remembered,

After dinner [one day in Chinon] the king went for a walk in the grounds [of the castle]. In that very place Joan tilted with a lance. When I saw she held and tilted the lance seemly, I gave her a horse. (Q 3, 92; D-T 5, 211)

Marguerite La Touroulde, with whom Joan had lodged in Bourges, paid the younger woman this compliment, "Joan on horseback handled a lance like an expert among the soldiers, all of whom were astonished." (Q, 3, 88; D-T 5, 209). These two remarks, expanded by future writers, became the source of enlarged stories. The *Chron. de Lorraine,* as usual more like fiction than history, transfers Joan's first action with a lance to the Duchy of Lorraine. Baudricourt has come with Joan to Duke Charles. Astonished when she assures him she *will* ride and show her skill with a lance, although she never did either before, the duke gives her a steed, armor, and a lance. Joan, spurning the stirrup, blithely leaps into the saddle and runs a faultless tilt to gain the fascinated approval of the assembled local nobility. Just a slender trifle for a saint in a saddle! (Q 4, 331). In a burst of eloquence Pius II gives her a spear, compares her to Camilla, and "mounts her on a spirited steed" which she made "leap, run, and curvet."

⚜ ⚜ ⚜

The Secret: We need not wonder about the detailed account here in which Joan divulges to the king the secret prayer he alone knew about. The sources for this, which the biographer for Louis XII admits he has not read, could be Pierre Sala and Alain Bouchard. Both give us gentle examples of naive hagiography, both propagate the pious fraud that Joan's parents took

*Vaucouleurs, the Gate of France through which, in February 1429,
Joan rode away to Chinon.*

Chinon, castle on the Vienne, where Joan first met Charles VII.

her to Charles VII. Nothing for them, it appears, succeeds like the successful unraveling of a royal secret, no matter how private the circumstances (Ay. 3, 277-8 and 287-8; Q 4, 268-71 and 279-80). There will always be zealous people not timid about undertaking the adventure of prying into others' affairs, even their prayers. We do not need a Freud to explain this proclivity.

⚜ ⚜ ⚜

"As many . . . as you can afford to pay . . ." Soldiers have to be paid. Joan knew this. *Les Payeurs d'Armes* by Frémont gives an interesting account of the sums received by different classes of soldiers.

3. CHARLES VII SENDS JOAN TO BLOIS . . .
(p 22 to p 26)

Troops and Materiel: Joan asked the King for troops and was given them to help her break the English blockade around Orléans. This is certain. The question, "How many?" introduces at once less certainty because her answer, given on Tuesday 27 February 1431 and preserved for us only in the Latin translation of the trial record, leaves us wide-eyed. The French minutes for this detail do not exist. In the translation Joan's surprising reply reads, "He gave me ten or twelve thousand men." (*X vel XII milia hominum*). If the accuracy of this figure is doubted, remember her judges were her enemies. The eminent theologian, Thomas Courcelles, who did the translation, was the most bitter of all. His hatred is steady, intense. To know what this means refer to his vapid remarks for her vindication. Father Paul Doncoeur's brilliant study, *La Minute française des Interrogatoires de Jeanne la Pucelle,* indicates where Courcelles stealthily altered the original minutes. The lost French original prevents a decision on the problem of the ten or twelve thousand troops. Abbé Dubois, who knew more about the siege than any other scholar, voices a judicious doubt about Joan's reply in his *Histoire du Siège d'Orléans,* ed. by Charpentier and Cuissard, 407-408.

77

Many witnesses for Joan's vindication hammer away repeatedly on two themes, her belief in the work she was to do at Orléans and her success there. When the din dies down the voice of François Garivel, a member of the King's Council in 1456, arouses our interest afresh. He tells us something new. We listen again. In that hopeful spring of 1429 he had talked to Joan in Poitiers. He questioned her about the number of troops she would need for Orléans. She answered, "If the King is willing to give me a body of troops *however small in number* (*quantalamcumque*), I have no doubt that the work will be done."

This sounds like Joan talking, calm, assured, confident. The phrase "ten or twelve thousand" does not.

"Small in number" may be an accurate estimate of the troops Joan was given. When she arrived before Orléans she had an argument with the Bastard, the "lieutenant general there for the King in matters of war." Joan's indignation over the route followed to the Loire "by way of the Sologne side" flared into words of reproach. The Bastard, not plagued with pompous self-importance, explained his decision generously.

The English are here in large numbers. The army escorting the convoy did not appear to me nor to the other captains *a sufficient force* to resist them and to ensure the entrance of the convoy on [the Beauce] side.

Ten or twelve thousand troops would have been more than a sufficient force.

Joan's military chaplain, the Augustinian friar Jean Pasquerel who enjoyed exaggeration, spoke clearly on this point in his statement for her vindication. "In comparison with the English the troops of the King [for the march to Orléans] were small (*modica*) in numbers." His words deprive us of the need of further comment on the "ten or twelve thousand." The strength of the English forces around Orléans has been studied alertly by Boucher de Molandon and Adalbert de Beaucorps in their earnest research, *L'Armée anglaise sous les Murs d'Orléans*. Louis Jarry's book has an equal interest, *Le Compte de l'Armée anglaise au Siège d'Orléans*.

⚜   ⚜   ⚜

Opinions: The King endorsed Joan. His counsellors approved her. That she was not accepted by all his advisers with equal enthusiasm is natural. She was an outsider, a girl. Her feminine presence created its own disturbance. Not that she ruffled the calmness of masculine emotions or mind. She was merely a woman, disturbance enough to upset the conservative. Echoes of distrust and disapproval are in the notes of the Dean of the Collegiate Church of St. Thibaud of Metz. His language is quaint, graphic:

The English held the siege before Orléans, a siege wonderfully nailed down (*clout*). Then the Maid asked and beseeched the King to be willing to find some of his people for her. "I will undertake, for the delight of God, to raise the siege, to battle the English. I have no doubt that I will halloo to victory." Then the captains of the king made derision and mockery, "Look, our valiant champion and captain! *She* will recover the kingdom of France?" They muttered against the King and his counsellors, all except the Duke of Alençon and a courageous captain of good will named La Hire. (Q 4, 327)

The testimony of Joan's young page, Louis de Coutes who idolized her, is more impressive. In 1456 he had not forgotten his pang of surprise in 1429,

From Tours Joan went to Blois in the company of the troops of the King. This group [of soldiers] at that time did not have the least trust in Joan, (*illotunc habebat minimam fiduciam in eodem Johanna*). (D-L, 5, 197).

This lack of confidence in Joan may have had its murky origin in the influence of the enigmatic Archbishop of Reims, Regnault de Chartres, who had presided over the commission of churchmen in Poitiers where it had been agreed that the King might make use of Joan's help. Toward Joan he had a diplomat's pitiless superiority. His letter to the people of Reims after Joan's capture is heartless, an expressive nod of adverse opinion more subtle than avowed hatred (Q 5, 168).

79

✤ ✤ ✤

Blois: Time and an explosion of fury during the French Revolution have destroyed all trace of Joan of Arc's days in the city of Blois. No chronicle even hints at the location of her residence. The *Chron. de la Pucelle* gives us a garbled relation of a short religious ceremony.

During her stay in Blois she had a white [the color of unbleached linen] standard made on which were images of our Holy Savior and two angels. She had this blessed in the church of Our Holy Savior.

In reality this standard was made in Tours. The chronicle must mean the smaller banner which her chaplain carried. Today a plaque near the castle marks the site of this little church wrecked by the enthusiasm of the French Revolution. Simon Beaucroix, the married cleric who gave his opinion of Joan for her vindication, remembered that she returned to Blois after the triumph of freeing Orléans. He does not say why. Today in Blois the most satisfactory evidence of Joan's presence in the city is the American tribute to her in the Public Gardens, an equestrian statue overlooking the river Loire, the gift of a New York philanthropist Mr. J. Sanford Saltus and his friends, dedicated 13 August 1923. This is a replica of the statue to Joan by Ann Hyatt (Mrs. Huntington) on Riverside Drive, New York City. The artist has captured in bronze one abrupt, taut split-second of a brusque stop, horse and rider tense, motionless before the decisive onrush.

✤ ✤ ✤

Joan's Letters: The cross with the words *Jesus Maria* on Joan's letter to the English incited the curiosity of her judges. On Saturday 17 March 1431, during the afternoon questioning, they asked her, "You mark your letters with the sign *Jesus Maria?* What does this mean?" Joan replied laconically, "The secretaries added them. Some said it was becoming for me to use these two words, *Jesus Maria*." This repeated question must have bored Joan, for two weeks before on Thursday 1 March they had asked her, "Is it your custom to begin your letters with the names *Jesus Maria* and a cross?" She replied clearly, "On some letters, Yes; on others, No!" Then she revealed a secret agreement. "At times I used the cross to warn those who understood [what it meant] *not* to do what I had written in that letter." The judges accepted this and went on to read to her the entire letter to the English. She gave them prompt answers to their prying inquiries about this. (Q 1, 83; T-L, 82).

The mistaken, commonly accepted notion, odd and beguiling as it is, that Joan of Arc did not write or read, suppresses for many all awareness of the number of her letters we know about. Some have been lost. Others remain in their original form or have been kept in documents that copied them.

THESE ARE THE LOST LETTERS WE KNOW DID EXIST.

1. To her father and mother begging them to forgive her for leaving home.
2. The letter she wrote from St. Catherine of Fierbois to the King in Chinon.
3. To the priests of Fierbois from Poitiers.
4. To the King during the siege of Orléans.
5. That third letter to the English.
6. Her invitation to the Duke of Burgundy for the King's Coronation.
7. One to Charles VII about Catherine de la Rochelle.
8. To the people in Tours asking them to give a wedding gift to the daughter of the artist who had painted her standard.
9. All the letters marked with the cross which meant, "Do not believe this or do it."
10. Doncoeur believed that a letter from Joan went with the gift of "a little ring" she sent to Anne de Laval early in June 1429 (Q 5, 109).
11. To the Bishop of Senlis.
12. To the people of Troyes.
13. To the King of Navarre.
14. To the people of Clermont-Ferrand.

THESE ARE THE LETTERS THAT HAVE NOT DISAPPEARED.

For the year 1429

1. The famous 22 March summons to the English.
2. A letter, again to the English, dictated by Joan to her chaplain, Friar Pasquerel, 5 May.
3. To the people of Tournai (now in Belgium) dated 25 June.
4. To the people of Troyes, 4 July.
5. To the Duke of Burgundy, 17 July.
6. To the people of Reims, 5 August.
7. To the Count of Armagnac, 22 August.
8. To the people of Riom, 9 November.

For the year 1430

9. The second to Reims, 16 March.
10. The much-disputed letter to the Hussites, 23 March.
11. The third to Reims, 28 March.

Not an overwhelming collection but one to pique interest.

4. ORLÉANS DELIVERED
(p 26 to p 30)

The Plans: The cleric, monk, or friar who wrote this *Life* knew less than little about the forts, bastiles, and boulevards the English constructed on each side of the river. Of all the books written about this siege not one is definitive. Each writer counts and totals the English fortifications to suit a personal preference. Our author is the only one to reduce them to four, two on each side of the Loire. We have not discovered the source of his balanced quota. He prolongs the attack on *The Tourelles* over a two-day period because Chartier does in his chapter 38. He rewrites the account of the war council from which Joan was excluded with pretty details that please his ingenious imagination. Chartier seems to be the only early chronicler to record this bizarre business. In chapter 37 his account is less gushy. An angry Joan makes no mention of her sex. Too indignant to sit down, she remains standing to say bluntly, "Tell me what you have approved and decided. I am keeping secrets much more important than this one of yours!" The truth is, she was. Joan never told anyone the secret she had revealed to the king. The *Bologna Manuscript* of 1569, "qui fut donné à Monsieur le Cardinal d'Armagnac . . . le jour de Notre-Dame XXV de mars MDLXIX," relates that Joan knew the decision of the captains even when she was excluded from their meetings (pp. 12-13 of the 1890 edition of André Du Bois de La Villera-bel). The *Chron. de la Pucelle* (Q 4, 227) and Pierre Sala (Q 4, 278) both remind us that Joan opposed plans of other military commanders. Secrets are not involved in either narrative.

Joan's Wounds: A caltrop caused Joan's first wound. This was an iron device adorned with sharp spikes. Thrown on the ground it impeded and injured mounted troops. On Friday 6 May 1429, during the attack on *The Augustins,* she stepped on one of these orb-like inventions and injured a foot (Q 4, 227). Next day she was wounded more severely, this time above a breast, by an arrow, not "in the leg" or "in the shoulder." She had predicted this accident. Her judges listened to her explain the circumstances during the trial on Tuesday 27 March 1431. They had asked her,

When you were on your way to relieve Orléans, did you not tell your people that you would take to yourself the arrows, shafts from crossbows, and stones [hurled] by the cannons?

Joan gave the assembled priests and prelates a firm denial.

No, I did not. Over a hundred or more soldiers were wounded there. This is what I told my people, "Do not have any doubts about it. You will raise the siege!" I was wounded in the neck [this is Courcelles's word for breast] by an arrow from a crossbow. St. Catherine amply consoled me. Within two weeks I recovered fully. The wound did not stop me riding horseback or doing my work.

Here the inquisitor broke in, "Did you have foreknowledge of this wound?" "Indeed I did," Joan replied. "The revelation came from my Voices, St. Catherine and St. Margaret. I told the King about it. In spite of my wound, I did not give up working."

In their remarks for Joan's vindication, the Bastard, then Count Dunois, and her chaplain Jean Pasquerel add some exciting details about the circumstances of this wound, details which the inquisitors in fulfilling their holy office would have discarded as unholy self-satisfaction on her part, had Joan told them. (Q 3, 8 and 109; D-L, 163 and 221.)

Towards the end of his chapter 38 Jean Chartier relates the incident of this wound. He adds mistakenly that Joan "did not retire or budge from the moat" where she received the injury. Our compiler with tender trust copies him again. There are accounts of this serious wound in the *Chron. de la Pucelle*, in the *Journal du Siège,* and in Eberhard Windecke. The German chronicler keeps closest to the facts as Jean Pasquerel tells them. Joan forewarned her chaplain on Friday evening 6 May, "To-morrow blood will flow on my body from a wound above my breast." This proved to be the truth. "The next day," he continues, "as she had predicted an arrow pierced her body above a breast."

To heal this jagged gash some soldiers suggested she apply a health charm they had and believed in. Joan refused. Instead she accepted a dressing of "olive oil and lard." Revived by prayer and this ancient remedy Joan "hastened back to the attack." (Q 3, 109; D-L 5, 221.)

She had a near escape from another severe wound at Jargeau when a stone struck the light helmet she wore and knocked her down. The Duke of Alençon recalled this accident. Fuller details are furnished by the *Journal du Siège.*

The Maid was so near the wall [of the city] an Englishman heaved a heavy stone of some weight on her head. It struck her such [a blow] she was obliged to sit down on the ground. Although this stone was a very hard mass it broke into very small pieces, hardly injuring the Maid at all. Displaying energetic courage, she sprang up quickly. (Q 4, 172)

Joan suffered another wound while battling under the walls of Paris. Again an arrow from a crossbow hit her, this time in the thigh. During her trial she told her judges on Thursday 22 February 1431 how this wound healed in five days. Joan's misfortune during the attack on Paris and her bitter lack of success there received widespread publicity during her lifetime and for decades after her death. A partial list of writers who tell of her reverses includes Chartier, of course; the *Journal du Siège;* Eberhard Windecke; the *Journal d'un Bourgeois de Paris;* the *Chroniques de Perceval de Cagny;* Philippe de Vigneulles; the Dean of the Collegiate Church of St. Thibaud of Metz; the Clerk of Parliament in Paris, Clément de Fauquemberque in his *Notes;* Walter Bower in the *Scotichronicon;* Monstrelet; and Pius II. The notoriety of failure! Philippe de Vigneulles regrets with sympathy, "Fortune turned her back on the Maid." The thesis that Paris could have been taken if Charles VII had not been there is easy to defend. Orléans celebrates the anniversary of its deliverance. Paris does not because the King for whom Joan continued her purposeful work destroyed her chance of activity by turning his back on his own good fortune.

5. JARGEAU
(p 30 to p 32)
[See also Appendix p 133]

Jargeau: This brief version of the taking of Jargeau away from the English, which they had held since October 1428, is in Jean Chartier, chap. 42, the *Chron. de la Pucelle,* chap. 50, and in Gaguin, Bk. X, fol. CXVIII. The surprise in each one of these accounts is identical. All three allow the siege of Jargeau to languish "eight days." The *Journal du Siège* is more accurate. In its relation the town fell within two days. The formal attack began on Saturday morning 11 June 1429, and after a ferocious assault Jargeau was taken on Sunday 12 June. Joan was in Orléans the next day. (Q 4, 13 and 235.)

When Dunois talked about this battle for Jargeau during his remarks for Joan's vindication he omitted all mention of an attack he had directed some time before without her help. In this earlier effort he had been repulsed. This is what he preferred to say:

After raising the siege of the city of Orléans the Maid with me and other war captains went to the King, then residing in the castle of Loches. We asked him to direct his troops to recover the towns and castles along the river Loire. We meant Meung, Beaugency,

85

and Jargeau. [With these places freed] he could go on to Reims for his consecration with greater security and freedom. . . . From that moment the King made every possible effort. He sent the Duke of Alençon, me, and other commanders with Joan to recover these towns and castles I have named. Within a few days, in fact, these places were brought back to the obedience of the King, through the influence of the Maid. (Q 3, 9-10; D-L 5, 164.)

This is an intensely felt compliment.

Suffolk: What is said here about the Earl of Suffolk and his brothers at Jargeau is accurate. The *Journal du Siège* takes the time to give their names. (Q 4, 170.)

There is a good story, perhaps apocryphal, about the Earl of Suffolk in the notes of the Clerk of the City Hall of La Rochelle. Realizing that he was about to be taken prisoner at Jargeau by the Duke of Alençon or by others of the French nobles present, Suffolk objected, "I will not surrender to you. I'd rather die first." Then he cried out with a loud voice, "I surrender to the Maid, the most valiant woman in the world. She has vanquished us all to our utter confusion." If the English chronicles of the fifteenth century had not been so niggardly with their information we might know the truth about this impetuous gallantry of the Earl of Suffolk. (*Revue historique,* mai-août 1877, p. 340). A French letter written before the end of June 1429 adds a superlative note of chivalrous courtesy to the Earl's action:

"At Jargeau the Earl of Suffolk on bended knee surrendered to the Maid." (Q 5, 121.) This is an eager imagination at work, the art of seeing the unlikely.

6. MEUNG-SUR-LOIRE AND BEAUGENCY
(p 32 to p 34)

Meung-sur-Loire and Beaugency: In the fifteenth century the military importance of Meung was in its fortified bridge across the Loire. Beaugency's importance was in its tall, strongly fortified castle impressive even today as lean, grim-looking remains. The swift sentences here about Meung and Beaugency, few because the sources are brief, come from hurried remarks in Chartier, chs. 42 and 43, the *Chron. de la Pucelle,* ch. 52, and Gaguin. If the compiler read Monstrelet's ch. LXI, he discarded its details.

Salisbury: Thomas Montecute, Earl of Salisbury, 1388-1428, had possession of Jargeau, Meung, Beaugency, and Janville before he laid siege to Orléans. Taken to Meung after his grisly injury during the siege, he died there on Wednesday 27 October 1428 (*Journal du Siège,* Q 4, 101). If any reader prefers the date "3 November," given in Dugdale's *Baronage of England,* 1, 653, he may have failed to notice in this account the remark, "He died two days after he was wounded." The time of the wounding was late Sunday afternoon 24 November 1428.

Salisbury, the great soldier, would have been a more worthy opponent of Joan of Arc, the soldier saint, than any other English commander of his day. Both had the same military talents—imagination, daring, skill, relentless drive—and the personality to inspire confidence. Salisbury's death rescued him from the humiliation of defeat at the hands of the Maid. Waurin, a soldier under him, wrote a sincere tribute to his memory. Any success of Joan of Arc against the redoubtable Salisbury would have provoked her contemporaries to praise more rapturous than she ever received. Waurin's sympathetic praise is touching:

He was accounted in his time through France and England the most expert, subtle, and successful-in-arms of all the commanders who had been talked about in the last two hundred years. He had all the virtues of a true Knight, for he was gentle and humble and courteous. He was liberal with all he possessed. He gave alms freely. To the lowly he was kind and full of sympathy. To haughty enemies he was like a lion or a tiger. (Waurin 3, 254.)

Insofar as a man's last will and testament expresses accurately his virtuous qualities, moral or natural, the terms in which Salisbury states his wishes about the disposal of his property after death, corroborate Waurin's eulogy. The *Testa-*

mentum domini Thome de Monte Acuto comitis Saresburie, a document rich in human interest, is in Prof. E. F. Jacob's superbly edited *Register of Henry Chichele, Archbishop of Canterbury,* vol. 2, 390-400. Joan of Arc, whose liberality to the poor and the lowly is told in Quicherat 2, 427, 438 and 3, 88, 464, would have loved and applauded Salisbury's generosity.

Patay: The account of the battle of Patay, more tense and vigorous than any other page our compiler wrote, comes from the three sources noticed above. The surprise of the French victory, its annihilation of a stalwart portion of English troops, literally stunned the chroniclers who tried to describe its details. All accounts are tangled. To arrange the movement of the sudden events of that day into a lucid narrative is no longer possible. Joan of Arc had predicted a moment of new grandeur for France. "Today's victory *will be* the greatest the King has had for a long time." (Q 3, 99; D-L 5, 215.) She did not say, "I will bring him victory." Today, however, England's most competent historian of the fifteenth century, gives this explosive hour to her.

Because she gave her opponents no time and no rest, Patay was Joan's battle, though she was only in the van with Arthur de Richemont the constable, while La Hire and Poton de Xaintrailles formed the spearhead for the main body under Alençon and Dunois. (Jacob, *The Fifteenth Century,* p. 247.)

Writers from Joan's day to the present, excited by the surprises of Patay, add an occasional misstatement to their narratives. The first to do this was Charles VII himself. He made the slight mistake, repeated by others, of placing the name of Sir John Fastolf in the list of the captured. In a letter to the residents of Tours, preserved in substance in the records of the Mayor's office of that city, we read:

To Stephen de la Fontaine, a royal messenger, who rode to Tours with a letter from the King, the sum of 6 *livres tournois* is given and paid by order of the people of Tours. This letter tells of the battle won by [our] leaders, the Duke of Alençon, the Count of Vendôme, and the Maid, against the English, our ancient enemies. . . . On the 18th day of the present month [of June] 2,500 English were killed or captured. Taken prisoners were [Lord] Talbot, [Sir John] Fastolf, [Sir Walter] Hungerford, [Sir Thomas] Rempston, [Lord] Scales and other captains. . . . And for this good news 6 *livres* have been given to the messenger . . . on the 22nd day of June 1429. (Q 5, 262-263.)

In her letter to "the noble, loyal French in the City of Tournai," written at Gien 25 June 1429, Joan announces the good news of Patay, includes Fastolf among the captives, and begs all the inhabitants of the city to "be ready to go to Reims for the coronation of the Noble King Charles" (Q 5, 125). Sir John Fastolf and his depleted contingent, deprived of their supplies and ammunition, retreated to Janville, a village "qui est assez bonne petite ville," in Waurin's words. Salisbury had taken the place on 20 August 1428. Now, with the gates of the village proudly closed by its people against him, Fastolf marched on to Etampes, at least 60 fatiguing miles from Patay, without rest or respite from French annoyance.

Eventually Talbot, the nominal commander at Patay, was ransomed. His own petition for the favor of having 8,000 marks brought from England to pay his ransom was allowed on 8 January 1430. (Stevenson, *Letters and Papers of the Wars of the English in France,* I, 422-423.) Talbot lived through twenty more years of conflict. Defeat and death were in wait for him at Castillon in old Gascony in 1453. He was then the Earl of Shrewsbury, and the battle he lost allowed the records of the Hundred Years War to be closed. Three years later Joan of Arc's vindication was proclaimed officially by the Church.

7. THE ROUTE TO REIMS
(p 34 to p 38)

The March to Reims: With more than usual carelessness the chroniclers crowd confusion into their accounts of the start of the march to Reims for the coronation. The more direct, the logical route north from Gien was by way of Montargis. After a feeble start this was abandoned. The explanation given is that some towns not far distant from Gien were displaying "the flag of St. Andrew," a symbol of adherence to England. This explanation is ludicrous for troops who had battered the English brutally at Orléans and deprived them, in that week of brilliant victories, of Jargeau, Meung, Beaugency, and Patay. There was money to be had for one of Charles VII's intimates by going west and north in a curved route leading to Auxerre.

The essential details and dates of the itinerary to Reims seem to be these:

Wednesday 29 June 1429, the cavalcade rides out of Gien.

Friday 1 July, Auxerre is stubbornly defiant.

Sunday 3 July, the town of St. Florentin yields loyally to the French.

Tuesday 5 July, the cavalcade reaches Troyes, a city doggedly obstinate.

Monday 11 July, this city capitulates after six days of opposition.

Friday 15 July, Châlons-sur-Marne opens its gates.

Saturday 16 July, the cavalcade arrives in Reims.

Sunday 17 July, Charles VII is consecrated in the cathedral.

The sources of Part 7 are Chartier, chs. 46, 47; *Chron. de la Pucelle,* chs. 57, 58; *Journal du Siège,* and Gaguin, Bk. 10, folio CXVIII.

⚜ ⚜ ⚜

Joan's Advice: Joan's eloquent little speech to the King, spoken to persuade him to decide to become energetic and to move toward Reims, is longer than any of her remarks on record. The ideas are hers; the words, only in part. The reference here to the Maid's religious fervor, frequent communion and confession, comes directly from Chartier, ch. 45 and the *Chron. de la Pucelle,* the last lines of ch. 55. Neither of these sources is responsible for the unexpected change of the subject to the amusing non sequitur, "Joan never did any tasks [expected] of a woman." This remark is not a gibe, merely a gauche distortion of an observation by Gaguin, who in folio CXVIII, lines 3 and 4, after talking about Joan's "purity of life" and her "holiness" in general concludes, "She neither acted as women do, nor talked as women do." (*Et nihil muliebriter agebat aut loquebatur.*) For women in general this is not a compliment. For Joan of Arc it is an expression of admiration, praise, courtesy, respect. She, although feminine, had for this clerical mind qualities worth noting. What Robert Gaguin, a learned, cosmopolitan churchman of his time, the Superior General of the Trinitarians or Mathurins, thought of women is patent.

La Trémoille: Unlike the chroniclers, the compiler neither points a finger of blame nor reproaches anyone by name for the shock of the stalemate before Auxerre. He is content to say, "With the connivance of certain ones close to the king" Auxerre was not disturbed. Chartier, the *Journal,* and the *Chron. de la Pucelle* are not so shy. For them the culprit is the King's most intimate adviser Georges de La Trémoille, the obese owner of the castle of Sully. For this disservice to his King, Georges de La Trémoille pocketed "two thousand gold crowns." (The *Chron. de la Pucelle* specifies "*deux mille escus.*") There is material in French archives for a revealing study of the career and character of this superior, aristocratic intrigant. What Professor E. Cosneau did for Richemont could be done for Georges de La Trémoille. The revelations could be as surprising and gripping as romantic fiction. His interest in money alone equals that of his contemporary, the Cardinal of Winchester, Henry Beaufort. A document of rare interest, almost unique in history, is the royal order Charles VII signed at Georges de La Trémoille's personal request in Poitiers on 7 May 1431, a short time before Joan of Arc was condemned to death, "to annul *all the excesses* Georges de La Trémoille had committed since the year 1416." This mandate was an attempt to put a white robe of innocence around the burly Peer of the Realm, a tragicomedy of regal favoritism. (*Les La Trémoille pendant cinq Siècles,* I, 192-195.)

Joan's Influence: If there were times when each soldier of the army of Charles VII had little to eat on the route to Reims, he was paid little enough money for his needs. *"Audit lieu de Gyen sur Loire fut faict un payement aux gens de guerre de trois francs pour homme d'armes, qui estoit peu de choses."* (*Chron. de la Pucelle,* 313.) Without the presence of Joan of Arc it seems certain that the courage and stamina of the soldiers marching toward Reims would have dissolved into a speedy disaster.

⚜ ⚜ ⚜

Le Maçon: Robert Le Maçon, shown here in a favorable light toward the Maid, hardly deserves this distinction. He was an intimate associate of Georges de La Trémoille. We suggest his intention was to denigrate Joan. Did he not wish to say, "She has involved all of us in this trouble, this impasse. Why not let the blame fall upon her? Let her talk and it will."? Usually called in the records of the time "the Lord of Trèves," he was ennobled in 1400 and died on 2 January 1442.

⚜ ⚜ ⚜

Troyes: The reference here to Charles VII's quick appointment of public servants to maintain law and order in Troyes and Châlons is an expanded version of a remark the compiler read in Gaguin, folio CXVIII, verso, lines 31-33. The *Chron. de la Pucelle,* 319-320 and Chartier 1, 96 refer briefly to the same decisions. The worthy Bishop of Troyes, who came out with citizens and soldiers to treat with the King about the terms of the capitulation of their city, was Jean Leguisé or Laiguisé, whose father had been one of the first of the city's celebrities to sign the articles of the disruptive Treaty of Troyes in 1420. The Notary (*Greffier*) of La Rochelle, pages 341-342, adds details to his account of the Bishop's diplomatic move that other writers neglect.

During her trial on Saturday 3 March 1431, in the mass of miscellaneous topics argued that day, Joan was asked abruptly, "What honors did the people of Troyes show you on your arrival?" Her reply was, "Honors to *me* at Troyes? None!"

La Charité-sur-Loire. Joan's prolonged efforts to recover this fortified town failed.

Statue of Joan on the Ballon d' Alsace between France and Germany. Mathurin Moreau, Sculptor.

8. REIMS, THE CORONATION
(p 38 to p 39)

Joan's Standard: The writing here has a quality of compression, a skillfully inspissated account of the coronation marred by one detail of absurdity, "the Maid bore the standard of the King." All his sources told him, "In the church of Reims [during the coronation] Joan the Maid held *her* standard in her hand." (Chartier; *Chron. de la Pucelle;* Gaguin. *The Notary of La Rochelle* gives us the same fact.)

Joan's judges twice during the trial sternly disputed her right to this honor. On Saturday 3 March 1431 she replied to their brusque query, "Yes, my standard was in the church at Reims. I believe it was rather close to the altar. *I held it for a little while.*" This destroys the pretense in pietistic utterances and writings that she stood all through the ceremony, from nine in the morning to two in the afternoon, beside the altar with her standard.

Saturday 17 March 1431 was a long day of questioning. Joan's judges sat and harried her in a morning and in an afternoon assembly. Late in the second session she was asked, "Didn't someone have your standard wave or stream [in the air] by the side of your King?" To this Joan said, "No, not to my knowledge." The irritable tension in the next question is clear. "Why was your standard carried into the church at Reims for the coronation rather than those of the other captains?" Joan rejoined, "It had been at the suffering, reason enough to have it at this hour of glory!" The judges gave up and swarmed out of the hall.

⚜ ⚜ ⚜

The Archibishop: Regnault de Chartres, Archbishop and Duke of Reims since 1414, had not been in his diocese for twelve years. In the words of Germain Lefèvre-Pontalis he was a "devotee of all diplomatic illusions," capable, indeed, but more politician than priest. Close to Charles VII, he felt safe after Joan's capture to suggest his dislike for her in a letter of intense relief, unctuously written to the people of his diocese in May 1430:

Joan the Maid is taken before Compiègne. She never accepted advice. She did what she pleased . . . God has allowed her to be taken because she gave herself up to pride and to the rich clothes she wore. "My will be done," not what God ordered her to do, was her rule. (Q 5, 168.)

Joan, the girl saint, was a dire distraction to the Archbishop who did not recognize her holiness. His unashamed, conscious prejudice overflowed from the depth of his unconscious antagonism.

9. CAPTURED AT COMPIÈGNE
(p 39 to p 46)

Explanation of Omissions: With an engaging candor that disarms criticism (he explains why he made the decision) the compiler passes over events in Joan's career from the coronation of Charles VII in July 1429 to her capture before Compiègne in May 1430. In this way, and his philosophy of history is his justification, he saves himself the discomfort of telling the details of her failure before Paris during September 1429 and her lack of success at La Charité-sur-Loire during the extremely cold weeks of November that same year. Bored and vexed at the inane pretense of court life at the castle of Sully-sur-Loire near Orléans she fled late in March 1430 from this fortress of the King's favorite, Georges de La Trémoille. In May she went to help her good friends of Compiègne and was captured.

⚜ ⚜ ⚜

Bishop Cauchon: At this point a bishop whose active opposition to Joan has darkened his fame enters her history brusquely. An adroit diplomat, intellectually brilliant, learned in law and theology, Peter Cauchon, the Bishop of Beauvais, although a menacing churchman, neither terrified nor intimidated her during the trial. Her last words to him, spoken in prison the morning she went out to die, were stinging and defiant, "Bishop, I die through you."

94

To understand him it is important to remember the position and function of many fifteenth-century bishops. Although a comparison between him and Henry Chichele, the Archbishop of Canterbury, would be presumptuous, such a study would be fruitful. They were contemporaries. Both were devoted wholeheartedly to the political prosperity of their country. Cauchon's country was England, by choice. Who dare say it was not by conviction? He believed in the Treaty of Troyes, he was a close friend of Henry VI and the Duke of Bedford and a member of the Great Council of Henry V and Henry VI in France. Two weeks before Joan was captured Cauchon was reconfirmed in this office of distinction by Henry VI. The fee was only part of the value of the position. The document of confirmation has more than an interest of curiosity.

HENRY, BY THE GRACE OF GOD, KING OF FRANCE AND ENGLAND, TO ALL THOSE WHO SHALL SEE THESE PRESENTS, GREETING

WE make known that in consideration of the good and loyal services the Reverend Father in God, Our Beloved and Faithful Counsellor, the Bishop of Beauvais rendered to my late and very dear Lord and Father—may God release him from punishment—since the final treaty of peace of Our Realms of France and England [Troyes, 1420] and renders to us at the present time, in our councils and in other affairs and concerns, WE, on the advice and decision of the members of our Great Council, assembled in our presence, have kept and do keep him in office as our Counsellor with the pay and allowance of one thousand *livres tournois* for each year of service.

Given in Calais, the 14th day of May in the year of grace 1430, and of our reign the 8th. [*Bib. Nat.,* Ms fr, 20881)

Three weeks earlier Henry VI, only eight years of age, had landed in France at Calais on St. George's Day 23 April 1430. Monstrelet tells us in the 87th chapter of Book Two, "The Bishop of Beauvais, Peter Cauchon, was there."

⚜ ⚜ ⚜

95

The Ransom: The offer of "10,000 *livres tournois*" or a king's ransom, made by Cauchon as the emissary of the English for the transfer of Joan of Arc to his protective custody was accepted, another proof of the persuasive eloquence of money. The Chronicle of Perceval de Cagny reports a detail about this diplomatic negotiation that, if true, was logical and helpful. The Bishop of Thérouanne, Louis of Luxembourg, "Chancellor of France for the King of England, went to his brother, John of Luxembourg, to convince him to accept the financial offer." (H. Moranvillé, *Chroniques de Perceval de Cagny,* p. 176.)

The wheel of misfortune began its slow, relentless turning against Joan. Under pressure from the Regent, the Duke of Bedford, the Estates of Normandy on 4 August 1430 in Rouen voted to disburse the enormous sum called for to pay for her release. Then Thomas Blount, treasurer in Normandy for the King, and Pierre Surreau, minister of finance there, in a document signed in Rouen on 24 October 1430 acknowledged the order from the King to disburse 2,636 *nobles d'or,* the said sum to be given and delivered to John Bryce, "the Custodian of the coffers of the King (*garde des coffres du roy*)."

On 6 December 1430 John Bryce in a signed receipt acknowledged that this transaction included the "10,000 *livres tournois* paid out for the purchase of Joan, the prisoner of war, who called herself the Maid." (Q 5, 190-192; J. Félix, *Inventaire de Pierre Surreau,* p. 149.) The wheel had stopped at the point marked "Death."

With the business of this bargain nicely adjusted to the desires of Bishop Cauchon and the scholarly sentiments of the University of Paris, Joan the pawn was moved in a roundabout way north and west from Compiègne to Le Crotoy near the coast before she was hustled into Rouen late in December 1430.

⚜ ⚜ ⚜

There is only one biography of the Bishop of Beauvais, *Pierre Cauchon, Juge de Jeanne d'Arc;* it was written by Albert Sarrazin and published in 1901. French scholarship seems ashamed of the Bishop. Interest in his life and ambitions is not equivalent to condoning his excesses. For an ambivert, his is a special case of failure. Because results have issued from our search for material to renew an interest in the Bishop, we hope to prepare a new biography of Peter Cauchon, who was more than just a "judge of Joan of Arc."

10. JOAN'S TRANSFER TO ROUEN
(p 46 to p 51)

Source of Information: The official record of Joan's trial of condemnation and its original French Minutes gave the writer of the *Life* the material he selected for his concluding sections.

The Duke of Burgundy, Philip the Good, needed Compiègne for a safe route north of Paris through Picardy into Flanders. This important city had opened its gates to Charles VII the year before. On Thursday 18 August 1429 the King entered in triumph. Beauvais, less than thirty-six miles away, capitulated, and its bishop, the redoubtable Peter Cauchon, moved rapidly to safety. Now a year later with characteristic energy and rapidity he rode into Burgundy's headquarters near Compiègne, where John of Luxembourg and John Holland the Earl of Huntingdon were giving Philip the Good strong but not effective support to retake the stubborn city.

⚜ ⚜ ⚜

Nicolas Rolin: Nicolas Rolin, the Chancellor for Burgundy, was indispensable to the duke in diplomacy, politics, and intrigue. At the Council of Basel he was to be a prominent bother. (N. Valois, *Le Pape et le Concile,* I, 112-115.) Today he is perhaps best remembered as a patron of the arts. He admired and aided Jan van Eyck, who repaid him by portraying him in a charming work now in the Louvre, *La Vierge au Donateur.* Arsène Périer's study, *Un Chancelier au XVe Siècle, Nicolas Rolin,* has not lost its value.

⚜ ⚜ ⚜

Triquelot: Nicolas of Mailly, mentioned in the text, has the distinction, in an age when men changed their allegiance lightly, of remaining steadfast in his adherence to the English cause in France. John of Pressy, a soldier and diplomat, was at one time a member of the Great Council of Henry VI in Rouen. The name of "Triquelot" is the only fact known about the individual who signed the affidavit. At a later date some eager searcher may come across details of interest about him. His signature is a reminder of the power of the testimony of an Apostolic Notary during the Middle Ages. The statement of *one* notary equalled the evidence of *two* other witnesses. A statement signed as this one is here voided opposing evidence presented in court. When Triquelot writes of "the *five* articles" instead of the three actually in the document he is signing, this confusion may be a slip of the pen.

The Letter of Henry VI: The forceful, even violent tone of the letter demanding the surrender of Joan to the Bishop of Beauvais reflects Cauchon's personality. The name "J. de Rinel" affixed to this letter is the signature of John Rinel, the famous French secretary of Henry VI at that time. He was related by marriage to Bishop Cauchon. His descendants had moments of acute embarrassment during Joan of Arc's trial of vindication. He had married Guillemette Bidault, the daughter of Jean Bidault whose wife's maiden name was Joan Cauchon. She was the sister of the Bishop of Beauvais. John Rinel, after a life of service to the Bishop and his intimate English interests, died in 1450, the year the first efforts to vindicate Joan of Arc came to a sudden standstill. It is possible to follow and evaluate the variety of work and service John Rinel did for his English employers by reading the documents he signed that are now included in Stevenson's *Wars of the English in France.* A detailed resumé of his life and his numerous missions in England are in Miss J. Otway-Ruthven's *The King's Secretary and the Signet Office in the XV Century,* a delightful example of assured scholarship. Further information on Rinel is in Charles de Beaurepaire's "Recherches sur le Procès de Condamnation de Jeanne d'Arc" in *Précis analytique des Travaux de l'Académie impériale de Rouen, 1867-1868.*

⚜ ⚜ ⚜

The Capture: Monstrelet, an eye witness, describes the tumultuous excitement and rejoicing of "the English, the Duke of Burgundy, and those of other camps assembled in very great numbers" to celebrate the capture of Joan of Arc. He explains their burst of satisfaction,

They were happier to have her than five hundred other combatants, because they had never feared and dreaded any other captain or war commander up to the present time as they had this Maid. . . . The Duke said a few words to her, which I do not very well remember, even though it is true I was present there. (Book 2, ch. 86.)

The tone of the historian's narrative attests the absence of abuse in word or gesture. If awe subdued invective, why be surprised that Monstrelet did not remember the Duke's "few words?" Philip the Good, never a man of many words, allowed his satisfaction the full scope of enthusiasm in a letter he wrote at once to the people of Saint Quentin:

TO OUR VERY DEAR AND GOOD FRIENDS, THE CLERGY, CITIZENS, AND INHABITANTS OF SAINT QUENTIN IN VERMANDOIS

Very dear and well-beloved friends, assured that you wish to hear the news from us, we inform you that this day, the 23rd of May, toward 6 o'clock in the afternoon, the enemies of the King [Henry VI] and ours as well, who were assembled in great power and supported in the city of Compiègne, before which we and the men of our army were camped, made a sally from the said town in force against our advance guard nearest to them. In this sally the woman, whom they call *The Maid,* was with many of their leading captains. In this encounter our fair cousin, John of Luxembourg, who was there present with others of our forces and some of the forces of the King (sent to us on their way to Paris) made a strong and bold resistance. Presently we arrived in person to find our enemies already driven back. It has pleased our Blessed Creator to allow and grant us a great grace—*The Maid* has been captured! Other captains, knights, squires, and soldiers with her were taken or drowned or killed, their names at this hour we do not yet know. Thank God none of our followers nor any of the followers of the King are killed or taken, and only twenty are wounded. This capture, we truly believe, will be welcome news everywhere. Now the error and foolish belief of those who approved and favored this woman will be recognized. We write you this news in the hope that it will give you joy, comfort, and satisfaction, and that you will thank and praise our Creator Who sees and knows all things. May it be His blessed pleasure to direct all our undertakings for the benefit of the King and his realm and for the relief and comfort of his good and loyal subjects. Very dear and well-beloved, may the Holy Spirit keep you in His Holy Care.

Given at Coudun, near Compiègne, the 23rd day of May 1430. By order of the Duke of Burgundy, Count of Flanders, Artois, Burgundy, and Namur.

These words probably say in full what in his excitement the Duke only expressed in a "few words" that same day when in Monstrelet's presence Joan the prisoner stood before Burgundy.

11. JOAN CONDEMNED
(p 51 to p 54)

The Betrayal: After Joan signed her abjuration, Nicolas Loiseleur, the priest whose treachery in her regard was exposed at the trial of vindication remarked, "Thank God, Joan, this has been a good day for you. You have saved your soul." To this Joan, showing her good common sense, replied, "Now then, among yourselves, as churchmen, take me to your prison, since I am no longer to be in the hands of these English." In spite of a promise and assurance given her, Bishop Cauchon broke in abruptly, "Lead her back to the prison from which you took her." This happened on Thursday 24 May. On Monday Cauchon and his clerical cohorts crowded into her dungeon to ask her again some of the questions she knew by heart. Joan as before replied with her brave boldness. On one point she said something new,

I would rather die than be kept in these chains. But if you promise to remove them and allow me to attend Mass and put me in a "gracious" prison (*en prison gracieuse*) and let me have a woman attendant, I will be good (*bonne*) and do everything the Church wishes and orders.

On Wednesday 30 May 1431, the day she was to die, Joan told those who came to the prison early in the morning to prepare her for martyrdom by fire, "Alas, if you had kept me in a church prison, guarded by churchmen, as you should have, this might never have happened. That is why here I appeal from you to God!"

Falsification of Minutes: Bishop Cauchon's official record of the trial does on occasion falsify the original minutes. The most interesting and flagrant example is the so-called abjuration. Joan signed a little document of six or seven lines. Cauchon allowed this to be altered and enlarged to five times its original length. His intention was not to be helpful or favorable to Joan. Another example is in the original text for Thursday 1 May which reports Joan's words, "Within seven years—and I know this by revelation—the English will lose all they have in France. This length of time makes me sad (*dolens*)." The official text has her say, "This delay *angers* me (*irata*)." On Monday 19 February 1431 all the judges in solemn assembly "took an oath to keep secret everything done in this trial." (*Tous les assistens jurerent tenir secret tout ce qui sera faict en ceste matiere.*) No word of this is in the official papers. Why did Cauchon keep it out? During her questioning on Thursday 22 February 1431, Joan explained, ". . . in Neufchâteau for fifteen days I lived with a woman named La Rousse. There I attended to the affairs of her home. I did not watch over her sheep or the other animals in the fields." This clear statement is enlarged and distorted in Article 8 of the *Seventy Articles* read to Joan on Tuesday 27 March 1431. The false additions are *underlined:*

ARTICLE 8. . . . in Neufchâteau Joan was *in service* at the house of a woman, *an inn-keeper* named La Rousse, *where women of evil life lived and where soldiers were accustomed to lodge in great numbers. During her stay at this inn Joan sometimes stayed with these evil women or led the horses to water in the meadows and pastures. There she learned to ride horseback and to use arms.*

When asked what she had to say to this plenitude of clerical falsification, Joan replied defiantly, "I refer to what I have said already [on Thursday 22 February and Saturday 24 February]. I deny the rest." To realize how often Joan objected to the *Seventy Articles* by saying, "I deny that entirely" or "I deny the rest," the whole accusation has to be read. A comparison of the *French Minutes,* only partially preserved, with the Official Trial Record reveals other falsifications.

⚜   ⚜   ⚜

According to the compiler of this *Life,* Peter Cauchon, the bishop who presided over and controlled the proceedings of the trial and its foreseen verdict left the scene before Joan was burned to death. This is contradicted by the 1452 testimony of the Dominican Friar, Isambard de la Pierre, one of the young priests with Joan to the last, who says almost laconically, "While Joan was dying, the Bishop of Beauvais, one of her judges, shed tears." Joan died on Wednesday, the day before the feast of Corpus Christi. The Bishop sang the Solemn High Pontifical Mass for the feast next day in the Cathedral of Rouen (*Archives de la Seine-Inférieure,* G. 33). We have no record of his thoughts or his sentiments on either occasion.

EPILOGUE
(p 54 to p 64)

The official record of Joan of Arc's trial of condemnation offers its readers two letters written over the signature of Henry

VI. The compiler did not reproduce the King's epistle to "the Emperor, Kings, Dukes, and Princes of Christianity," dated 8 June 1431. (Q 1, 485-489; T-L, 423-426; Ch. I, 402-404.)

⚜ ⚜ ⚜

Letter, 28 June 1431: The first flagrant falsehood in the letter given here is laughably absurd: "She made the demand both to have and to display the truly noble and surpassing Royal Arms of France." A prudent reader asks at once, "What reference is there in the trial record about this coat of arms?" For this question Joan's words are important. The judges asked her on Saturday 10 March 1431, "Didn't you have an escutcheon and a coat of arms?" Joan explained,

No, I never had either. But my King gave a coat of arms to my brothers, that is *a shield azure with two fleurs-de-lys or and between them a sword point upward.* I described these arms to a painter who asked me what arms I had. These arms were given by my King to my brothers to please them, without any request from me and independent of any revelation.

Joan's attentive judges took her explanation without the least demur and at once asked their next question, "What sort of a horse were you riding the day you were captured, a charger or a hackney?"

Joan's account of these arms given her brothers says nothing about "a crown of gold encircling the tip of the sword." This detail, denied by Joan on the instant, is first mentioned in this letter and repeated in Article 58 of the *Seventy Articles of Accusation* already discussed. This is another deliberate falsification, one that has captured the popular fancy, in light-hearted defiance as it were of Joan's exact description. Not one of the official manuscripts with the transcript of the judges' questioning includes the mention of a crown in Joan's replies.

All through his long career this century's most distinguished Joan of Arc scholar, the eminent Jesuit, Father Paul Doncoeur, tried without success to persuade French writers and publishers to respect Joan's explanation on this point. He failed, perhaps, because the appeal of royalty is too rich. In respectful and affectionate appreciation of the friendship of Father Doncoeur, the illustrations of the coat of arms given to Joan's brothers conform, in this little book, to her description.

There is a cry of cold fury in the letter, a distressing admission of military defeat: "This woman disrupted all possibility of real peace by reviving a languishing war." The real meaning here is, "This woman deprived us of victory." Had Joan not believed in the work given her or not been willing to accept her private revelation, the English would have won the war. Her work was to see that they did not.

The honor and respect or "veneration" shown Joan by the people was broached during the trial. The question about this came on Saturday 3 March 1431. "Didn't you realize the fervor of those who believed in you, when they kissed your hands or feet or your garments?" To this Joan answered,

People were happy to seek me, many people. And they kissed my clothing only insofar as I could not prevent them. The poor came cheerfully because I did not cause them any confusion but did all in my power to assist them and provide for them.

Henry VI's letter distorts this by repeating a sentence in *Article 2* of the *Seventy Accusations,* "The accused permitted people to venerate and adore her." Joan's denial said, "About 'adoration' —it was neither my wish nor my doing if people kissed my hands or my clothes. As far as it was in my power, I kept them from doing it." Popular esteem and respect springing from sincerity had not been the judges' experience.

There is a cry of cold fury in the letter

Without fear of contradiction this letter could state categorically, "This woman refused and rejected the authority of our Holy Father the Pope." None of the Prelates, Dukes,

Counts, and Nobles to whom this letter was addressed were likely to read the manuscripts of the trial's proceedings. Today everyone may read Joan's expression of complete understanding and submission to the Pope's spiritual authority. On Saturday 17 March 1431, she heard this question,

In your mind are you obliged to speak the truth fully to the Pope, the Representative of God [on earth] about all he might ask you relating to your faith and the state of your consience?

Joan answered at once, "I demand that I be taken into his presence in the Church and there I will reply to all questions I am bound to answer."

All through the weeks of the trial Joan's references to the Pope rankled in Bishop Cauchon's combative spirit. He was heard to say, "Shut up! Shut up!" on an occasion of annoyance. In answer to a final appeal, which one of the judges never wearied of repeating during the trial, to submit to the Church, Joan again a long step ahead of them elected to give preference to the Pope. Thursday 24 May 1431 was the moment of Joan's abjuration. "As I have already told you," repeated Joan, "about my submission to the Church: let all my words and deeds be submitted to Rome to our Holy Father the Pope to whom—but to God first—I refer them. As for my words and deeds, I said and did them by authority from God." Cauchon did explain, weak as the reason was intellectually and morally, why he paid no attention to Joan's demands to be taken to the Pope, "As to our Holy Father, it is impossible to go and bring him here (*pour aller querir*). *He is so far away.*"

The reality of Joan's stubborn religious belief, her firm faith in submitting her words and deeds to the Pope, makes her theology clear. Some modern writers, Shaw included, seeing her through the mist of an emotional attachment, distort her into their image of someone who had repudiated the Pope.

Letter, 12 June 1431: This letter must have had its inception in an amorphous fear. Certainly there was no reason to fear Charles VII. We have been asked often, "What was the King who owed the security of his realm to Joan of Arc doing the day she died? Where was he?" Charles was in Chinon, where he first met Joan, writing a letter of royal approval and thanks for the "good services Arnauld Guilhem, sire de Barbazan" had rendered him and his kingdom. We believe this embarrassing irony of history has not been pointed out before.

The "General Council" mentioned in this "Letter of Guarantee" means the Council of Basel which began under difficulties on 23 July 1431, less than two months after Joan's death. Evidence that the opening of this Council was in the thoughts of the churchmen interested in Joan's trial was brought out during her process of vindication. In his 1450 testimony Isambard de la Pierre said he begged Joan to submit her opinions "to the Council of Basel." Joan agreed. Cauchon, in a rage, ordered her words stricken from the record. Jean Beaupère, a priest of Rouen assiduous at Joan's trial, in his 1450 testimony for her vindication said he knew nothing of her "final repentance." He had left Rouen "on Monday 28 May to go to Basel as a representative of the University of Paris."

In the imposing array of names of the members of the Great Council of Henry VI who signed this letter only two are English ecclesiastics, neither of whom lived to hear of Joan's vindication. William of Worcester's Latin *Annales* recorded a terse notice of the death of each:

1447. Died Henry Beaufort, the Cardinal of England, brother of Henry IV, on the 12th day of April.

1449. On the 4th day of the month of December this year, William Alnwick, Bishop of Lincoln, died in a London hospital.

When he signed this letter William Alnwick was the Bishop of Norwich.

John de Mailly, Bishop of Noyon, lived to testify for Joan's vindication. He said, when shown a copy of this "Letter of Guarantee" on 2 April 1456,

I believe, indeed, that I was one of those mentioned in this letter but my memory is vague. I am sure, however, that the Bishop of

Beauvais did not pay for the expenses of the trial. I believe the King of England paid them. The English bore the whole cost of the trial.

By what means did the representatives of Pope Callixtus III succeed in finding a copy of this "Letter of Guarantee?" The answer is lost in secrecy. This "guarantee of protection" was never needed. To have its futility flaunted in public was a curious reversal of its original intention. When it did its part in 1456 to shed a brighter luster on the vindicated name and reputation of Joan of Arc, it exposed an unexpected stealth of anxiety and fear cringing in the conscience of Peter Cauchon. The Bishop's life is a tale of ambition and decay. History gives Joan of Arc what he craved for himself—success and fame.

Time has confirmed the compiler's conviction, "I found no event so remarkable or memorable as the story of Joan of Arc, nor one more deserving to be written down and to be kept as a lasting memory."

THE FIRST CHRONICLE TO RECORD
JOAN OF ARC'S EXPLOITS

A NOTE OF INTRODUCTION

[Credit for the discovery and proof of the importance and the priority of this anonymous *Chronicle* in relation to Joan of Arc belongs to a scholar of the past century. Learned but modest about his achievements, he usually signed his articles "F^x B", for Félix Brassart. Some years ago in the Congressional Library in Washington we came across his revealing article, "La Mission de Jeanne d'Arc résumée par un Chroniqueur wallon contemporain, 1429-1431," signed with his initials, in a bound volume of the magazine, *Souvenirs de la Flandre Wallonne*, Tome premier, Deuxième série, Douai, 1881, pp. 143-167. This was the first indication that a fifteenth-century manuscript in the Bibliothèque Nationale, today listed as number 23018 in the French section, contained a contemporary account, apparently the first ever written in a chronicle, of Joan of Arc. It was formerly in the Paris monastery of that branch of the Franciscans called *Cordeliers*, and from the knotted cord or cincture they wore, this manuscript is named *The Chronicle of the Cordeliers*, incongruously, for it is not a history of this order.

Quicherat, ever alert for material that had escaped his researches for his 1841-1849 collections, discussed this find in the *Revue historique*, vol. 19, May-June 1882, pp. 72-83. This was the last reference to Joan the great scholar wrote, for he died in Paris on 8 April 1882. (*Jules Quicherat, sa Vie et ses Travaux*, by Robert de Lasteyrie, Paris, 1883.) During 1886 Siméon Luce published his *Jeanne d'Arc à Domremy*. Without a nod of awareness to Félix Brassart, he included in the book's *Supplément*, pp. 336-344, most of what MS 23018 has on Joan of Arc. At least this was an opportunity for new readers to become aware of the interest of the *Chronicle*. Ayroles in his volume 3, *La Libératrice*, pp. 437-54, 1897, has the valuable section on Joan rendered into modern French. Again Félix Brassart escapes mention.

What appears to be the first printing of a portion of the manuscript is in L. Douët d'Arcq's edition of *Monstrelet*, at the end of the last volume. (6 vols., Paris, 1857-62). These pages, not concerned with Joan of Arc, relate to events from 1400 to 1422. Even when Brassart's original article with its Joan of Arc pages from the manuscript was reprinted as a pamphlet of 24 pages its anonymity was maintained.

⚜ ⚜ ⚜

Whoever wrote this manuscript 23018 was Burgundian in point of view and sympathy, not French. His style is that of a native of Picardy. His handwriting is an easily recognizable cursive script of the early fifteenth century. Brassart suggests that he may have composed his chronicle in Lille. Although a partisan of Philip the Good, he was not unfriendly to Joan of Arc. His work begins, as many in the Middle Ages do, with a brief report of Creation.

In the beginning after God had created heaven and earth, darkness and light, and the four elements separate one from the other, He formed diverse created things to adorn the world—herbs, trees, fishes, birds, and beasts. Many prefer to say that the world was created in the month of March, which, according to the Hebrews, is the first month of the year. [Nisan, Esther 3,7; Neh. 2,1.]

After these created things I have already mentioned, on the 6th day of the beginning of the world, God created from the earth, in His own image and likeness, our first father, Adam, who was, indeed, a perfect man the first day he was created. It was as if he were already 30 years of age and had not just been formed in an earthly paradise, which is in a place called *The Garden of Damascus.*

In spite of this not very encouraging beginning and other portions tedious to read, the anonymous author's pen comes alive, like a journalist's, when he begins to write down what rumor or report brought him about people and events in his own day. He began by putting down, like a compact headline, the indications of time! IN THE YEAR 1429 *(De l'an mil iiij xxix).*

[In the chronicler's recording of the events after Joan's assault on Paris, there are paragraphs noticeably out of place. We prefer not to change his order but to allow his history to stand just as he wrote it. Ayroles has pointed out the superlative value of letters in this portion of the chronicle which help to explain the baffling conduct and the awkward hesitations of Charles VII during the attack on Paris. These letters do not concern Joan of Arc directly nor mention her. We have not included them in the translation. Our intention is to center interest on "a young girl born in Lorraine, the daughter of a poor farmer." Joan of Arc is an innovation in history. Because of her coming, the plans and ambitions of Henry V, bequeathed to his infant son, slowly dimmed. Time saw them disappear. What remains is only a memory.]—*The Authors*

IN THE YEAR 1429

At this time a young girl born in Lorraine, the daughter of a poor farmer, came to the Dauphin [Charles VII]. She had herself called *Joan the Maid.* In her native village she guarded sheep. This Maid, who appeared very innocent in word and manner, always let it be understood that she was divinely inspired and that she had the duty under this divine inspiration to place the Dauphin in possession of the kingdom of France and to have him obeyed throughout the [realm]. She insisted on this so much to her father and her friends that she was taken to the Dauphin by one of her brothers with other people whom she found to join her escort.

She spoke so well the Dauphin kept her at his court and set her up in great state. This astonished most of his people because they considered Joan just a simple and foolish girl. Retained by the Dauphin and maintained in this high position, Joan boldly asked to be mounted and armed as a soldier for war. At the same time she promised to work wonders. Her request was granted. She was no sooner armed than she set out along the route [toward Orléans]. Before long a great host of men-at-arms assembled to raise the siege of Orléans after the failure, as it is said, of the negotiations [between the messengers from Orléans and the Duke of Burgundy]. The Maid joined and associated herself with this assembly of men-at-arms and raised a standard on which she had inscribed the name JESUS. She continued to claim that she was sent by God to place the Dauphin in possession of the kingdom of France.

At the beginning of the month of May in the year 1429 the siege of Orléans was raised by the power and the might of the forces of the Dauphin. The Maid was there and she *did* begin to work wonders by word and by deed as she had promised. In fact she did so well that this was the beginning of her great renown. Those of her party placed high hope in her. There in Orléans the fortresses of the English were captured and burned. There the English experienced heavy damage and great loss of life. After the

siege of Orléans was lifted the Dauphin of France rose to
the height of his power when his troops and the Maid
recovered Beaugency, Meung, Jargeau, and several other
fortresses from the English. Lord Talbot, with several
other lords and captains, who were captured, were held as
prisoners for a long time, in particular Talbot. Taken at
Jargeau [a mistake for Patay] he was handed over to Poton
de Saintrailles when the city fell by storm and assault.
Early in the afternoon of the 18th of June the troops of the
Regent [Bedford] in combat with the forces of the Dauphin
in open country were completely defeated near Janville
and Etampes. The Regent retreated to Paris with the rem-
nant of his army. The Lord of l'Isle Adam [Jean de Villiers]
shortly after was sent [as captain] to that city.

⚜ ⚜ ⚜

With the Maid in arms and always near [to help] him
with a great number of men under her command, the
Dauphin of Viennois acquired new courage. He began to
conquer fortified places and regions through the exploits
and the prowess of the Maid whose fame was spreading
everywhere. A mere word or summons from her was
sufficient to determine a fortress to surrender. Her marvelous deeds [inspired] the belief and the hope that here was
something divine. She did astonishing feats of arms with
her bodily strength. She handled the thrust of a lance with
very great vigor and, as was evident every day, she availed
herself readily of this strength.

What is more she admonished her troops in the name of
Jesus. In sermons she had the people invited to return to
Him and to obey the Dauphin. Ultimately rumor spread
the fame of her deeds as something miraculous far and
wide, even to Rome. Hearsay had it that whenever she appeared before a fortress the people within, no matter how

strong their determination had been before her arrival not to surrender either to the Dauphin or to her, became, all of them, mute and feeble and had no power to defend themselves against her, so they gave up at once. This happened at Sens and Auxerre and other fortresses. Even though the King did not take possession of several places, his money purchased provisions [for his troops].

Another marvel took place at Troyes in Champagne, a city always so loyal to Burgundy it had promised to hold the place for him and not to surrender. And yet advised and called upon to surrender by the Maid, it gave up straightway without striking a blow. This astonished everyone, most of all the princes and nobles allied to the Duke of Burgundy, who were greatly perplexed.

[The next paragraph in the manuscript is irrelevant to the narrative.]

At this time after the surrender of Troyes the Dauphin came into possession of many towns and fortresses through the power of the Maid, who by these deeds took away all the credit from the captains and men-at-arms of her forces. On this account none of them was the least bit happy! She brought all the country above the Loire under obedience [to the Dauphin], that is, all the fortified places of Auxerre and Champagne except those fortresses held by Perrinet Grasset who, unwavering in his determination never to surrender or yield obedience to the Dauphin, inflicted heavy damage and loss on his followers.

⚜ ⚜ ⚜

At this time the Duke of Burgundy sent his ambassadors to Reims to invite the city to remember its oath to remain faithful to him until peace was established and to urge the inhabitants to remain under obedience to their king [Henry VI] and to him. This they promised to do. Meanwhile the Dauphin and his army marched forward toward Reims. To oppose this advance of the Dauphin, Bedford the Regent had assembled an imposing army in June [1429]. Now to this army he joined all the troops he could gather, that is, those who escaped and were saved [from the defeats] at Orléans and Janville. While the Regent was getting this army under way, the Dauphin and the Maid, successful in one conquest after another, came to Sept-Saulx, in the vicinity of Reims. The Dauphin sent a summons to the inhabitants of Reims to open their gates and render obedience to him. (Remember, they had promised the ambassadors of the Duke of Burgundy, as I have said before, to remain firm in their opposition to the Dauphin.) Now when the people of Reims listened to this summons to submit to the Dauphin, they gathered in council. Their decision, made quickly, was to open the gates of the city and render obedience to the Dauphin as their rightful sovereign. This was done.

The Archbishop of Reims [Regnault de Chartres], Chancellor of the Dauphin, entered the city the 15th day of July. On this occasion he was accompanied by a very large retinue. He was received and welcomed with much pomp and ceremony.

For his entrance into Reims on the 17th day of this month of July the Dauphin was attended by the Count of Richemont, the Duke of Alençon, the Count of Vendôme, Charles de Bourbon, the son of the Duke of Alençon, with the Lords La Trémoille, Bosqueaux, Grand Pré, Graville, and Gamaches, Poton de Saintrailles, the Lords Gaucourt and Dampierre, Etienne de Vignolles called La Hire, the Maid, and other captains and nobles, in all a very great number. The Dauphin's army was strengthened by the arrival every day of men-at-arms and the common people in force.

He was anointed and crowned that day in the church of Reims by the Archbishop.

The following Thursday he was at St. Marcoul to heal the sick, [The Abbey Church of St. Marcoul of Corbeny]. The Maid, arrayed in white armor, rode on horseback before the King, with her standard unfurled. When not in armor, she kept her state as a knight and dressed as one. Her shoes were tied with laces to her feet, her hose and her doublet shapely, a hat was on her head. She wore very handsome attire of cloth of gold and silk, noticeably trimmed with fur.

From Reims the King Charles VII sent emissaries to Laon. Although he did not go there, this city, like the others, opened its gates and assured him of their allegiance. On the 22nd day of the month of June [July] La Hire, appointed the new Bailiff of Vermandois by the King, assumed the function of this office "In the Name of the King." Henry David was made Provost and Captain of Laon, where, as I have already remarked, the King did not go. He passed by St. Quentin which neither offered nor refused him obedience. He went to Soissons and from there to Senlis, which, following the example of other cities I have mentioned, surrendered to him. But the city of Noyon refused the oath of fealty. The king tarried a short time in Senlis. From there he dispatched his army and the Maid to St. Denis. After a little while he arrived there. However, he did not have himself crowned [in its Abbey Church].

⚜ ⚜ ⚜

He sent the power [of his army] against Paris several times. During one of these attacks in the vicinity of St.

Laurent, the Duke of Alençon and the Maid were repulsed and beaten by the forces defending Paris. Six or seven hundred of the king's army were killed. Then [the King] withdrew to Senlis [St. Denis]. On another occasion an assault was made against Paris from the heights of Montmartre. The Maid worked wonders! Her words and her confidence gave courage, even boldness, to her troops for this encounter. Under the walls of the city she was wounded in a leg by an arrow. Repulsed, she and her whole army failed in their effort. The city of Paris was guarded and defended by the Lord of l'Isle Adam, who had been sent there by the Duke of Burgundy with a strong force. With him as defenders of the city were the Lord of Saveuses and Hues of Lannoy as well as the Bastard of Saint Pol, the Bastard of Thyan, and others.

⚜ ⚜ ⚜

At this time the Regent took the field with his army along the river Seine. With him were the Cardinal of Winchester and [Robert] Lord Willoughby, recently come from England with 6,000 troops.

Before the King Charles VII moved toward Paris there had been a meeting between the Archbishop of Reims, Georges de la Trémoille, Poton de Saintrailles, and La Hire on the one hand, and on the other, John of Luxembourg, [Nicolas Rolin] Chancellor for Burgundy with the Lord of Croy and the Lord of Lourdin de Saligny. But, after all, no agreement was reached either about a truce or for peace. This meeting was held near La Fère.

When the adherents of Charles VII realized that Paris refused obedience to the King, they sent emissaries several times to Compiègne, which surrendered and swore allegiance to King Charles. William of Flavy with a strong assignment of troops was appointed captain of the city.

Then these fortresses surrendered—Creil, Pont St. Maxence, Château-Thierry, Lagny, and several others. But Breteuil and Chartres held steadfast [for Henry VI] as did Pontoise, Mantes, Vernon, the Bridge at Meulan, Charenton, Vincennes, and others. War continued to devastate the whole realm of France.

⚜ ⚜ ⚜

Then on the 3rd day of the month of August [1429] the Regent left Paris with an army, after sending a letter to King Charles on the subject of his wars and victories. Here is the letter.

WE, John of Lancaster, Regent of France and Duke of Bedford, to you, Charles Valois who were in the habit of calling yourself the Dauphin of Viennois and now without reason say you are the King of France,

You, by leading the plain people to believe that you have come to bestow on them peace and security, have organized new offensives—and done this unjustly—against the Crown and the Sovereignty of the very high and excellent Prince, my Sovereign Lord, Henry, by the grace of God, the true, legitimate and rightful King of France and England.

This is not and will not be tolerated! Consider the means you have used and still use to delude and abuse the ignorant. You are aided and abetted most of all by superstitious and depraved individuals, by that disorderly and deformed travesty of a woman, who dresses like a man, whose life is dissolute, and by that mendicant friar, a seditious apostate, rather than by the force and power of arms. Both [of these], as we have been informed, are according to Holy Writ, abominable to God! You have taken possession of several cities, towns, and castles in the region of Champagne and elsewhere that belong to the King [of France and England]. You have induced and constrained those who live in these regions to become unfaithful and perjured subjects, by compelling them to break and violate the final peace *(la paix finale)* between the kingdoms of France and England, a peace agreed to under oath by the Kings of France and England then alive [in 1420] and by the great Nobles, Prelates, and Lords and by the Three Estates of this Realm.

WE, to safeguard and defend the true rights of our Sovereign the King, and to drive you and your army from these regions and domains, with the help of the Almighty, have taken the field in person and are on the march with all the might that God has given us. As you have known and do know, WE have pursued you and will continue to pursue you from place to place in the hope of finding you and giving battle to you, something WE have not been able to do so far, because you have stolen away and still steal away. This is why WE who long with our whole heart to end this war, call upon you and demand that you—if you, a prince, are a friend of honor—take pity and compassion on the poor Christian people who, because of you, have been inhumanly dealt with, trampled on, and abused. For their sake, end this war. Let them be sheltered from such affliction and sorrow.

Designate an acceptable and sensible locality in this region of Brie, where you and I are at present, or in l'Ile-de-France, which is near us both. Appoint a suitable day in the near future . . . If on that day and in that place you will agree to appear in person, escorted and aided by the deformed travesty of a woman and by the apostate friar, both already mentioned, and accompanied by all your followers who have committed perjury and the other accomplices whom you wish and are able to find,

WE, and may this please Our Lord, will make our appearance, that is to say, the King will be present in our person.

Then and there if you wish to suggest or to put forward something *(quelque chose)* for the cause of peace, our ear will be attentive and WE will attempt all that can be and should be done by a Catholic prince. . . .

Let us know promptly, without further delay and without loss of time in writing or in quibbling, what your intention is. Should the fault be yours that great evils and difficulties arise, such as the continuation of this war, pillages, killings, and the holding of people for ransom,

WE take God as our Witness and WE solemnly declare before Him and before all men, that WE are not the cause, that WE have done and are doing our duty, that WE hold fast to and will hold fast to all terms of reason and honor. Let this in the first place be accomplished by the methods of peace; then, if not, by the outcome of combat, in virtue of the rights of princes, for there is no other way of procedure between powerful princes.

In testimony of this we have had these presents sealed with our seal. Given in this place of Montereau-où-fault-Yonne, the 7th day of August in the year 1429.

Signed: By His Lordship, the Duke of Bedford, Regent of the Realm of France.

Notwithstanding such a letter King Charles neither accepted nor cared to accept this offer for a conference or a combat. He kept on conquering other places. . . . At this time the city of Beauvais with a portion of that province of France yielded obedience to him. The inhabitants went through the region taking towns and castles, not by force of arms but by negotiation. . . .

IN THE YEAR 1430 [and 1431]

On the feast of St. George, the 23rd day of April [1430] the young King of England sailed into Calais. As befitted his royal dignity, he was escorted by forty-eight ships. These brought two thousand troops and a vast supply of cattle and provisions destined for Normandy. The men-at-arms were assigned to garrisons in Normandy and in France. Some were sent to Compiègne and other places where they were needed. The young king sojourned in Calais until the month of July. Thence he journeyed to Abbeville and from there to Rouen where he remained for a long period to time. . . .

On the 21st day of May [1430] Compiègne was besieged from the left bank of the river Oise [from the West]. The Earls of Huntingdon [John Holland] and of Arundel [John Fitzalan] had arrived with numerous companies of English soldiers. During the long time they encamped before the city they built bridges, bastiles, and other fortifications to hem in the place [on this side]. While the siege continued, large forces from the city made several sorties against the besiegers, for, without any danger they could receive reinforcements and supplies from the other [east] side of the river, that is, the Paris side. They had constructed a strong fortification of earth on their side of the river. In this way they had the advantage, for they came and went in and out of the city as they pleased by means of its trenches. There were in this fortress several rooms and lodgings for their men-at-arms who inflicted heavy losses on the Burgundians and English [on the other side of the river]. More often when these sorties were made they were directed in particular against the English rather than against our soldiers from Picardy.

The Maid had come into Compiègne with a large body of troops. She made a sortie every day to confront the assailants. She did work wonders both by word and example, inspiring her men to do their duty well, so well that on the 27th of May [the 23rd] during a sortie she directed, she and the lieutenant William of Flavy, at that time captain of Soissons, performed prodigies of valor. Their troops numbered fifteen hundred men. John of Luxembourg happened by chance to come in time to the support of the English under violent attack. The tumult and the clash of conflict were cruel. But toward the end [of the day] the Maid was taken and held captive by the Bastard of Wandonne and Antoine de Bournonville, both of whom were of the company and the household of Luxembourg. At the same time the lieutenant [William of Flavy] was taken and several other men-at-arms. The rest of the insurgents were driven back into Compiègne.

✤ ✤ ✤

The capture of the Maid was noised about excitedly everywhere. For Burgundy and his adherents it was a great joy. For the others, a great sorrow, because their hopes were in her, while the former held her in suspicion. Ultimately she was taken as a prisoner to Beaurevoir, where she was detained for a long time. By her ingenuity she sought to escape through a window. What she used to lower herself broke. From high up she fell to the ground and almost broke her loins and her back. After this injury she was sick a long time. When she recovered, she was handed over to the English. The negotiations for this [transfer] involved an agreement about money. Afterwards she was taken to Rouen for her trial, a prolonged case. At last she was condemned to death. I will tell all about this later on in its proper place, when I have time. [He never did.]

On the next to last day of May [1431] Joan the Maid was burned to death in Rouen. First of all she had been condemned to prison [for life] because she had retracted her errors as the result of a noble sermon preached to her on the subject of her conduct, a sermon delivered in the presence of the Regent of France [Bedford] and of several high princes and prelates. The members of the Great Council of King Henry VI were there, as well as all others who were desirous of hearing this sermon. But when she realized she was to be obliged to dress as women do, she remembered her past and said she preferred to die as she had lived. So she was condemned to be burned to death.

The ashes of her body, gathered in a sack, were tossed into the river Seine. This was done so that no attempt could ever be made, nor even a proposal be suggested, to use them for sorcery or any other mysterious evil.

COMMENTS ON THE CHRONICLE

The sentence introducing Joan both in this *Chronicle* and in the *Life* resembles nonidentical twins. The chronicler wrote, "En ce tamps, arriua deuers le daulphin une josne fille, nee en Loeraine et fille dun poure laboureur, laquelle se faisoit nommer Jennette la Pucelle et auoit garde les brebis ou village dont elle estoit nee . . ." Similarities are *underlined* in the version of the compiler of the first *Life*. "Or *en ce temps* avoit *une jeune fille en* pays de *Lorraine,* aagee de dix huit ans ou environ, *nommee Jhenne,* natifve d'une paroisse nommee Dompre, *fille d'ung laboureur* nomme Jacques Tart, qui jamais n'avoit faict aultre chose que *garder* les bestes aux champs . . ." Details added by the writer of the *Life* come from his familiarity with the record of the trial which the chronicler never saw.

⚜ ⚜ ⚜

The pretty story of Joan the shepherdess originates in this chronicle with these words, "In her native village she guarded sheep." Today this widespread myth is almost devoutly cherished, as if some intrinsic moral or spiritual excellence belonged to it. Why dream of bringing it to an end, especially in these days when more disturbing deposits of conservatism need to be carted away? During 1455-1456 thirty-four witnesses gave their recollections of Joan's youth to the representatives of the Pope's delegates, who questioned them in Domremy, Toul, and Vaucouleurs. They remembered Joan helping her father and brothers with farm work. She could plow, hoe, spade, and harrow. Sheep are not mentioned. Long ago in 1895 a courageous French writer, Léon Mougenot, gave the title, "Plowing" (*A la charrue*), to the first chapter of his book, *Jeanne d'Arc.*

Even though he was a native of Joan of Arc's part of France, no one listened to his statements against the myth.

❦ ❦ ❦

Perrinet Grasset or Gressart, introduced into the text after the mention of Troyes, was an audacious freebooter and a skilled commander. In 1423 he took La Charité-sur-Loire away from Charles VII's adherents and made it his headquarters. For three weeks during the bitter cold weather of December 1429 Joan tried to wrest the place from him and failed. Through military ability and craftiness he held the fortified town until 1440. (L. Jeny and P. Lanéry d'Arc, *Jeanne d'Arc en Berry*, p. 86.) Monstrelet records his activities. No respecter of persons, he extorted heavy ransoms. Georges de la Trémoille paid him 200 *ecus d'or* to free a servitor on 31 May 1426. On 26 July of that same year 10,000 *ecus d'or* were handed over for the ransom of Georges de la Trémoille himself. Detained a second time, in 1432, this wealthy, corpulent nobleman gained his freedom after 18,000 *couronnes d'or* exchanged hands. (*Les La Trémoille pendant cinq Siècles.*) Not blessed with children Perrinet lavished his affections and his funds on his nieces, one of whom married a Spanish soldier of fortune related to the Borgias, nicknamed *l'Arragonnais*. This able adventurer, François de Surienne, became an indispensable support to Perrinet Grasset in his diplomatic and military intrigues. (A. Bossuat, *Perrinet Gressart et François de Surienne.*)

❦ ❦ ❦

When the chronicler lists "the son of the Duke of Alençon" among those who attended Charles VII for his entry into Reims, he is repeating false rumor. Alençon married Jeanne of Orléans, daughter of the captive Charles of Orléans, on 29 August 1423. Perceval de Cagny says the date was a Sunday. In 1429 no child of this marriage was old enough to carry arms and assist at the ceremony of the coronation.

❦ ❦ ❦

A 1961 book by C. W. Lightbody, *The Judgements of Joan,* discusses the *Chronicle of the Cordeliers* without giving credit to Félix Brassart. This may be because Anatole France did not. Pages 70-71 in this recent book seem a slightly distorted reflection of a paragraph in the Introduction to the more renowned author's *Life of Joan of Arc* (Eng. trans., p. XIX). In the newer book the writer "takes leave" of the chronicler "with a citation of his spirited description of Joan's entry into Compiègne the first time" and adds the names of Joan's retinue for the occasion. A search for these names in the chronicle leaves one dispirited. They are not there. They seem lighthearted inaccuracies. In the chronicle itself the description of Joan "with her standard unfurled" pictures her entry into St. Marcoul with the king after Reims. After his coronation Charles VII visited the Abbey Church of St. Marcoul in the town of Corbeny to "touch for the king's evil" those afflicted with scrofula. One witness for Joan's vindication, Husson Le Maître, a tinsmith and a friend of Joan of Arc's family, came to Reims for the coronation. He relates, "Joan saw the King to Reims, where I met her. From there the King went to Corbeny." A serious study of the strange tradition of healing power in the royal touch against scrofula in general, with special reference to this belief in France and England, is in Marc Bloch's *Les Rois thaumaturges.* This visit to St. Marcoul is noted by chroniclers as diverse as Chartier, the *Journal of the Siege,* Monstrelet, Jean Le Fèvre, Pius II, and Perceval de Cagny. This last added details of interest:

The King was in Reims until Thursday [21 July 1429]. On that day he had dinner and supper in the Abbey of St. Marcoul, where he slept that night. The keys of the city of Laon were brought to him there.

⚜ ⚜ ⚜

Félix Brassart drew attention to the challenging letter of sarcasm Bedford wrote to Charles VII. He noted how Monstrelet (in chapter LXV of Book 2), by changing one word and one phrase in this letter, turned its meaning in a different direction. First, the original calls Joan "disorderly and *deformed*" (*difformée*). In Monstrelet this becomes, "a woman of *evil repute*" (*diffamée*), a more vicious insult. Second, the phrase, "*rather than by the force and power of arms*" (*que de forces et puissances d'armes*), in the original, taunts Charles VII for accepting help from such a woman and such a friar instead of acting like a man and fighting his own battles. This becomes in Monstrelet a subordinate clause that destroys the vigor and venom of the original sarcasm. Monstrelet flattens the meaning to, "You are aided and abetted by the woman and the friar, *who* by the force and power of arms . . ." (*QUI de forces et puissances d'armes*). As Brassart concludes, "The lesson of the anonymous author is better." (*La leçon de l'anonyme est meilleure.*) The caustic sneer of the original is lost in Monstrelet.

"That mendicant friar" abused here was known as "Brother Richard," a Franciscan Cordelier, an emotional, popular preacher, who was perhaps an ambitious meddler. His name was brought into Joan's trial on Saturday 3 March 1431. Joan, in answer to questions, explained that she had never seen him until she met him at Troyes on her way to Reims. She did not know if he ever carried her standard but she did know that he and Catherine de La Rochelle were both "very dissatisfied with me." Joan had refused to fall in line with their schemes and suggestions. The loss of Joan's letter to Charles VII about Catherine de La Rochelle is a deprivation. It would be instructive and amusing to read what Joan had to say of "this Catherine, who is a fool, a mere cipher, and a liar." Joan told her to "go back to her husband and her children." In this letter there could have been an equally direct opinion of Brother Richard. Joan's mind and judgment were rich in psychological realism.

The exact date of Joan's arrival in Rouen as a prisoner is not known. She was in the city on 28 December 1430. The official letter of the Chapter of the Cathedral of Rouen granting Bishop

Cauchon the right to bring her to trial, *sede vacante*, is dated, "In the year of Our Lord 1430, the 28th day of the month of December." Of Joan it says, "She has been brought to Rouen and there placed under secure guard." She remained under guard until death released her.

APPENDIX

I

JARGEAU

The town of Jargeau on the Loire repays a longer and more detailed visit than it usually receives from tourists, including those enthusiastic either about Joan of Arc or Suffolk. For this reason we add this appendix. Had the judges at her trial been less favorable to the English and to Suffolk, their commander at Jargeau, we would know less about Joan's ways of thought, feeling, and quick decision. Although official priority of command was not hers at Jargeau, she won the day by her intelligent daring and tenacity against what the *Chronique de la Pucelle* describes as Suffolk's "very fierce and bitter defence." The best account, because it is discriminating, of Suffolk's tragic career and shocking death has been written by Percival Hunt in his *Fifteenth Century England*.

Charles VII kept away from Orléans and Jargeau after these places were returned to him. The reason is obscure. We offer no explanation. What may be said is that he had visited and knew well Orléans, Jargeau, Meung-sur-Loire, and Beaugency. In 1420, the year of the Treaty of Troyes, while he was Dauphin, he made Jargeau the headquarters of the loyal French troops under Philippe of Orléans, the Count of Vertus, younger brother of the Duke of Orléans, still a prisoner in England. Credited in his day with military genius, this young nobleman was to be the commander of the French forces preparing to relieve Melun, then encircled by Henry V and the Duke of Burgundy. The Dauphin visited Jargeau on 6 August 1420, returned on 17 August, and remained there until the 21st. He was at Meung on 28 August where he learned for certain that the Count of Vertus was desperately ill. Philippe of Orléans died in Beaugency on 1 September. When Joan of Arc came did her success revive Charles VII's memories of that desperate year? Did he remember and dread that her exploits might end as his hopes did when the young count died in 1420? (Beaucourt, *Charles VII*, 1, 47 and 209-212.) It is an irony of history that Charles VII was in Jargeau when he heard the numbing news of Joan of Arc's capture before Compiègne (P. A. Leroy, *Jargeau*, 198).

It is evident from the questions asked her about Jargeau during the trial that Joan's judges had a dossier on her part in the taking of the town for the King. On Tuesday 27 February 1431 the day's questioning ended with this probe into a decision she was accused of making: "Why didn't you consent to a working arrangement with the [English] commander at Jargeau?" Joan replied briskly, recalling the unfruitful ruse of Suffolk who hoped for the arrival of more troops under Fastolf, "The English asked us to delay [our attack] for a fortnight. We refused." In her words this blunt refusal had a sequel, two alternatives offered the English. The first, a decision agreed to by the commanders, allowed the Earl of Suffolk the chance to move his troops and with them their horses, if they departed "on the instant." The second was Joan's more logical decision: they were free to go in safety *if they left their arms behind*. To stay meant capture during the siege.

The ranking French commander at Jargeau was the Duke of Alençon (Q 3, 98; D-L 5, 214, "*eodem tempore erat locum tenens pro rege in hujusmodi exercitu*"). In 1456, when he testified for Joan's vindication, Alençon spent a good deal of time talking about the details of the attack. He remembered how the Earl of Suffolk had had his request for a delay cried aloud (*fecit clamari*). He remembered his attitude toward the appeal. "To this," Alençon said, "I paid no attention." In other words he gave this request for a truce the flattest possible refusal, silence. When this remark is placed over against Joan's detailed report to her judges in 1431, a reader has to decide which version to accept. In 1456 Alençon's memory may have been blunted by distractions. His mind was on other matters. He was preparing plans of treason.

To call him "the commander-in-chief" at Jargeau and for the other engagements during the swift and destructive campaign along the Loire creates a difficulty. The title connotes a degree of authority invested in an individual neither possible nor acceptable at this time in fifteenth-century France. He was the "locum tenens," the lieutenant representing and acting for the King. What this amounted to is not impressive, since Charles VII, in contrast with Henry V, was not personally active in military operations. The superficial assent to Alençon's position in the army is emphasized by La Hire's individual decision to talk with Suffolk before the assault (Q 3, 95; D-L 5, 213, *relatum fuit quod La Hire loquebatur cum domino de Suffort*).

Here we must return to Joan on that day of complicated questioning, Tuesday 27 February 1431. Not interested in military minutiae the judges changed to a topic closer to their theological competence. "Did you have any consultation with your counsel, that is, your Voices to find out if you should or should not give [the English] this delay?" Joan may have smiled or shrugged as she replied, "On this point? . . . I do not remember." Here that long day's questioning ended.

On Saturday 3 March 1431 the trial judges brought up another perplexity in relation to Joan and Jargeau. This time it was about the heavy stone heaved from the ramparts, the hard boulder that went to pieces as it struck Joan full on the head. Perhaps, in the clerical mind, a link between the devil and this inversion of the natural order might be established. The question Joan heard was, "At Jargeau what was *that thing* you wore behind your helmet? (*derrière son heaume*) Was it something round?" Again Joan may have smiled as she answered, "By my faith, there was nothing!"

The third reference to Jargeau came later the same day. This relates to the bold visionary, Catherine de La Rochelle, who was with Joan there at Christmastime in 1429.

The fame of Jargeau, recorded by friend and foe, spread quickly over Europe. Monstrelet, certainly not a friend, in his Ch LXI wrote admiringly, "The French conquered the town by their valor. . . . Their terrible and marvelous assault lasted a goodly enough time." A German letter written late in June 1429 antedates Monstrelet. Quicherat, vol. 5, p. 350, published the part of this account time has preserved. Whoever wrote this letter in France to a friend in Germany dared to say, "This assault, the like of which was never seen before, was terrifying and devastating." Its odd, medieval German states, "*Was also ein grülich* (graulich) *jemerlich* (jämmerlich) *sturm, das me dann ein wagen getragen mag.*"

Robert Blondel, the learned Norman priest whose Latin is a delight, in his *De Reductione Normanniae* (*The Recovery of Normandy*) written in 1450 does not neglect Jargeau. He crowns Joan of Arc with an aureole of glory for her prowess there. "She, the Warrior Maid, was most strenuous." (*haec strenuissima bellatrix*.) Quicherat in 1845 ventured the prediction that Blondel's work "probably will never be published." He was mistaken, for in 1863 the distinguished Anglican scholar and priest, Joseph Stevenson, who became a Jesuit later, edited and published in England the full text of Blondel's history in his *Narratives of the Expulsion of the English from Normandy*, pp. 1-239. The quotation above is on p. 189. (Information on Joseph Stevenson is in *Great Historical Enterprises*, by David Knowles, pp. 105-6.) The most glowing modern telling of the victory of Jargeau is that of an English writer, Milton Waldman, in his *Joan of Arc*, pp. 138-142.

An American scholar's tribute to Suffolk, a skillful evaluation of "the changing views of Suffolk through four hundred years," is in Percival Hunt's *Fifteenth Century England*, pp. 99-121, a book written with affection and entire knowledge of the century, dazzling for those siding with France, depressing for the English and their friends, because, as Professor Hunt says simply, "Joan of Arc came."

2

AMBROSE DE LORÉ, *ca. 1396-1446*

The unknown author of the first *Life of Joan of Arc* gathers together and repeats in his narrative a few names of the military associates of Joan of Arc, namely, the Bastard of Orléans, Gilles de Rais, La Hire, and Ambrose de Loré. There are many volumes and studies on the enigmatic Gilles de Rais. La Hire has not been neglected; the latest book on the Bastard of Orléans was published in 1961, *Le Beau Dunois et son Temps*, by Michel Caffin de Mérouville. For an unexplainable reason Ambrose de Loré is slighted and forgotten. In Henri Chapoy's *Les Compagnons de Jeanne d'Arc*, a detailed volume of 445 pages, he is given only one paragraph. Not to fill this void but to suggest that it is worth doing, we have compiled this outline for a biography of one of Joan of Arc's close friends ignored by historians and writers.

❧ ❧ ❧

The Duke of Alençon in his testimony for Joan of Arc's vindication, given in Paris 3 May 1456, makes two specific references to Ambrose de Loré. He remembers that Charles VII had sent him to Yolande of Aragon, the King's mother-in-law, to discuss details about a convoy going with supplies into Orléans. On his arrival he found Ambrose de Loré, interested in the same task, there ahead of him to supervise the shipment of wheat. This first mention indicates Loré's energy in deeds. The second tells us something of his concern with thoughts. "What Joan did at Orléans," Ambrose de Loré said to me on several occasions, "was almost like a miracle, acts done less by human than by heavenly means." This opinion, according to Alençon, was held by other captains and commanders who had taken part in the deliverance of Orléans. However, Loré's repetition of this point of view seems to have impressed the Duke more than the thoughts of the others.

⚜ ⚜ ⚜

Ambrose de Loré's career, both before and after his association with Joan of Arc, is encrusted with the rust of time. Like Joan's sword from St. Catherine de Fierbois it deserves brightening. A medieval battle was a violent man-to-man encounter, a macabre game of polo without fixed rules, won by overwhelming your opponent. If you could outwit him, that was a brilliant advantage. The English enjoyed this advantage repeatedly, as at Crécy, Agincourt, Verneuil, and "The Battle of the Herrings." The French seemed determined to maintain a high average of defeats or disasters. It is painful to read Bishop Basin's reiterated explanation, "lack of order and military discipline . . . without discipline and ignorant of the use of their weapons . . . the pride and presumption of the Scotch [their allies]." (Thomas Basin, *Histoire de Charles VII*, ed. Samaran, I, 89, 93, 95.) Before Joan's coming Ambrose de Loré and the loyal French knew less of success than of defeat. In spite of this, Loré's career is worthy of notice.

⚜ ⚜ ⚜

The conjectural date of Ambrose de Loré's birth is 1396. Of humble origin, he was born in Loré, a hamlet in the medieval Duchy of Maine. With logical frugality the inhabitants there today are more interested in their orchards of pear trees than in the heroic companion of Joan of Arc. Domfront (Saint Front) was then and is now the nearest town. Built, as many medieval frontier fortresses were, on the heights above a river (here the Varenne), the place and its eleventh century church, Notre-Dame-sur-l'Eau (Our Lady on the Water), restored after the war damage of 1944, are worth an attentive visit.

The opinion of the few fervid French writers who claim without a word of evidence that Ambrose de Loré was at Agincourt, 1415, can be discarded. That battlefield is too far to the northeast. We do not know where he first felt the stinging excitement of approaching combat. As we would say today, his career began and gathered fame in the "western sector" of the Hundred Years War, that is, in Maine and parts of Anjou and Normandy.

Jean Chartier's *Chronique de Charles VII,* chapter 3 and the *Chronique de la Pucelle,* chapter 3, project Ambrose de Loré on the stage of war during October 1422 at Fresnay to help dislodge the English from this strongly defended place. Failure plagued the French again. Loré hastened back to his headquarters in the picturesque fortress of Sainte Suzanne. These efforts of Charles VII's loyal adherents were motivated by the death of the great Henry V, 19 September 1422. Later that same autumn at Bernay, "qui fut pleine de grande richesse," (*Chronique de la Pucelle,* 186), in a series of skirmishes spread over two days, the French, "filled with military ability" (*remplis de science militaire*) and inflamed "with a bellicose fury" (*avec une colère bellicueuse*) wrenched victory from the English. (Chartier, pp. 15-17; *Geste des Nobles,* chapter 194.) Ambrose de Loré was there to receive this compliment, "a very brave knight in arms" (*un très brave chevalier en armes*).

The year 1423 was a desultory one, until in July at Cravant just south of Auxerre, too far in the East for Loré to take part in the defeat, the English under Salisbury stupefied the French by another resounding victory like Agincourt. In the West, too, war never relaxed. What Chartier calls an *incident* added éclat to Loré's fame and encouraged the super-cautious Charles VII to be hopeful—on paper. William de la Pole and his troops had gone down into Anjou from Normandy. He captured the castle of Segré. With his booty—cattle, prisoners, and hostages to guarantee the payment of ransom—he marched straight north again toward another castle at Gravelle. French forces with Ambrose de Loré had gathered at the village of Bourgneuf.

At this point in the pages of the chronicles a puzzle appears, the name of the hamlet where the opposing armies collided. It is misnamed in Chartier, in the *Chronique de la Pucelle,* and in Cagny respectively as BROISSINIERE, BROSSINIERE, and BROUSSIGNIERE. Modern scholars misname it too. Vallet de Viriville says BROUSSINIERE; Jules Le Fizeler, BROSSINIERE, and Germain Lefèvre-Pontalis, BRESSINIERE. The correct name is BUSSONIERE, southeast of Bourgneuf on the road to St. Ouen. The evidence is two-fold, geographical and documentary. Geographical because this village still exists. Documentary because Guillaume Charrier, the Minister of Finance for Charles VII (*receveur général de toutes finances*), in his accounts lists this detail:

By letters patent of the King dated 27 October 1423 the sum of 4,050 *livres tournois* is to be paid out to aid in the construction of a chapel where the battle of BUSSONIERE was fought last September.

If you enjoy searching through old books as we do, you will discover this precise information in an aged but still authoritative history, G. A. de la Roque's *Histoire de la Maison d'Harcourt*, 1662, II, 496. No vestige of the chapel remains. Perhaps it was never built. A monument to recall this moment of grandeur, this triumphant victory of long ago, when France desperately needed the encouragement of its success, could be built today.

The English took Le Mans during 1424 as a postscript to Verneuil. In the defense of Ste. Suzanne, where he was captain of the fortress and the town, Ambrose de Loré's skill with artillery (all the chroniclers note this expertness) almost foiled the daring use of new English cannons directed by the great Salisbury. Several witnesses who spoke for Joan of Arc's vindication recall her expert talent in the placing of artillery. Some modern writers express chagrin, others surprise at this ability of the Maid. The explanation is not difficult. Owing to her intelligence and her youthful energy, she learned quickly and well from Ambrose de Loré and others like him.

During these years the destructive reach and the wrecking touch of artillery increased the hazards of war. In France under Charles VI the title "Master of Artillery" was given to Jean Petit on 7 October 1418. What he did to glorify his title is not recorded. Charles VII while Dauphin gave a grandiose label to the same office. On 1 October 1420 he endowed a loyal member of his royal household, Pierre Bessonneau, with a new title, "Master General and Inspector of Artillery" (*général maître et visiteur de l'artillerie*). For twenty years, until he resigned on 27 December 1444, in favor of Gaspard Burreau, he bore the hardship of his office. History gives us one meager mention of his work for Joan of Arc. During September 1429 he built the bridge Joan and Alençon needed to bring up reinforcements for the attack on Paris. To thwart their hopes and plans Charles VII, in royal secrecy, had it destroyed. (Bib. Nat. MS français 2342, folio 32.)

For a while during these complex and tragic years the chroniclers to whom Ambrose de Loré was merely a "vassal and servant of the Duke of Alençon" (Jouvencel), ring down the curtain of history on his activities. In 1427 he is again on scene operating in the west of France out of Sablé to harass the English in French strongholds they were holding precariously, as La Hire was doing in the east of the country. He retook Sainte Suzanne from John Fastolf and routed the English at the village of Ambrières (Beaucourt, II, 29 and 44). In the same year Alençon, a captive since Verneuil, came out of prison at Le Crotoy, where Joan of Arc was to be imprisoned on her way to Rouen.

❧ ❧ ❧

[Ambrose de Loré's military association with Joan of Arc, indicated briefly in the *Life,* need not be repeated here.]

❧ ❧ ❧

After Joan's martyrdom Loré acquired a special measure of fame during April 1432. He had risen in rank to be "the Marshal of the Duke of Alençon." (Chartier I, 135-137, emphasizes the title three times.) With violent persistence the English for two days attacked Saint Céneri (Celerin), an intricately fortified site rising on three sides out of the swift-running river Sarthe. Loré, wounded and captured—he evaded his guard and escaped—was a driving force in the victory. (Chartier I, 134-147 and Robert Gaguin, Bk 10, folio 121.)

During September of that same year Ambrose de Loré projected a daring and delightful foray on Caen, far to the north. The city, enjoying the excitement of the annual fair, was thronged to the limits of excess. The press of this swarm kept the gates of the city immobile (*On ne pouvait clore ni ouvrir les portes de cette ville.* Chartier, I, 151). With considerable booty and an assorted array of prisoners, including "presque tous les notables gens de la ville," Loré and his troops re-crossed the river Orne to safety. Chartier joyously relates:

On the opposite side of the river there was a cross. Here Ambrose de Loré halted his whole company with their prisoners. Trumpets sounded this proclamation:

BY AUTHORITY OF THE KING OF FRANCE AND THE DUKE OF ALENÇON THE THE PUNISHMENT [FOR DISOBEDIENCE] WILL BE HANGING

1. Release immediately all priests and churchmen held as prisoners.
2. Release immediately every captain and commander having a safe conduct from the King of France.
3. Release immediately all old men, young children, and poor working men.
4. If there be those who have anything to say for themselves, let them come forward promptly to the Marshal, Ambrose de Loré, at the foot of this cross.

This genial account, with its unexpected details of humane tenderness, is told at length in Chartier, I, 150-153. Gaguin, folio 121 verso, retells it in a lively Latin version, before which he affixes one laughing word—RIDICULUM, *A Droll Story.* In this narrative there is some evidence of the facets in Ambrose de Loré's character: daring, a sense of humor, sang-froid, an awareness of the young and of the poor working man.

During the year 1434 he was occupied with the fortunes of war that fluctuated around two fortresses, St. Célerin and Sillé-le-Guillaume. He and Jean de Bueil were dared by the English commanders sometime during September 1435 to advance and fight at a spot designated by the English on the road near St. Denis between Paris and Rouen. Loré and Bueil accepted the taunt, engaged in a combat, and routed their opponents.

From a military command in the field Ambrose de Loré was promoted to a position of political and military prominence in Paris during 1437. Charles VII took the city in 1436 as Joan of Arc had predicted but delayed his triumphal entry into the capital. Richemont, acting for the king, instituted Ambrose de Loré Provost of Paris, 23 February 1437. (Archiv. Nat. Y1, folio 278 r.) The King confirmed the appointment on 11 March 1437 (Archiv. Nat. Y4, folio 29 r). The problem of housing in Paris then was as perplexing as it is now. The King dismissed Loré's difficulty by giving him a residence that had belonged to the Bishop of Thérouanne, Louis de Luxembourg, a fervent admirer of the English, their chancellor in France, now fled to England where he died as Bishop of Ely. This palace, known as the *Hôtel de la Grange aux Merciers,* was near the gate of St. Antoine (the transaction in full detail is on record in the Archives of the Minister of Foreign Affairs in Paris, vol. 20, folios 127, 128, 129). On 5 April 1438 he was asked to do the impossible, that is, to curb and destroy bandits and brigands all over France. By royal authority he was declared "juge et réformateur sur les malfaiteurs du royaume, en quelque jurisdiction qu'ils se retirent." (Vallet de Viriville, *Charles VII*, 3, 399.) His old military acumen helped bring an end to the long desperate siege of Meaux on 12 August 1439. The English had held the city since 1422 when Henry V needed five months to take it. This was Ambrose de Loré's last display of skill and ingenuity in war.

He died in Paris during 1446. He may have been fifty years old. The *Journal d'un Bourgeois de Paris* tells us, "On the vigil of the Ascension [1446] the Provost of Paris, Ambrose de Loré, Baron of Ivry, was buried. He loved the common good less than any other Provost before him these 40 years." It is well to remember that this *Journal* was kept by a sour-tempered Frenchman, an Anglophile who could not tolerate the adherents of Charles VII. He has, however, a civil word for Loré's wife. "Of all the women of Paris [she] was the most beautiful and virtuous." In the tone of a modern scandal sheet he pens this tirade against the husband:

He was so lecherous, it is said, and it is true, that he had three or four mistresses, mere women of common property. He tolerated such women of folly everywhere, too many of whom were in Paris, because he was a coward. All the people held him in bad repute, for one could hardly ever have justice before the law, so strong was his support of them. They and their pimps! (ed. Tuétey, 383)

This is an enemy's revenge after an adversary's death. With Ambrose de Loré's morals we are not concerned, nor do we believe the smear of slander. Equally unacceptable is the halo of sanctity affixed above his head by a modern writer, the Vicar General of the diocese of Laval, Canon Cesbron, who wrote in 1929, "Ambrose de Loré's memory is without a blemish!" (*Jeanne d'Arc et le Bas-Maine*, p. 28.) Reality is wedged somewhere in between these extremes.

No *Life* of Ambrose de Loré has ever been published. The one promised in 1909 by the *Président de la Société historique et archéologique du Maine,* the learned Robert Triger, was evidently never finished (see his *A la suite de Jeanne d'Arc, ses Soldats et ses Amis du Maine,* Le Mans, 1909, p. 7, note 2).

We offer Loré's memory this small tribute because he knew Joan of Arc, worked with her, and expressed his appreciation of her.

BOOKS MENTIONED IN THE COMMENTS

Ayroles, J. B. J., *La Vraie Jeanne d'Arc*, 5 vols., Paris, 1890-1902.

Basin, T., *Histoire de Charles VII*, ed. C. Samaran, 2 vols., Paris, 1933.

Beaucourt, G. du Fresne de, *Histoire de Charles VII*, 6 vols., Paris, 1881-91.

Beaurepaire, C. Robillard de, "Recherches sur le Procès de Condamnation de Jeanne d'Arc," in *Précis analytique des Travaux de l'Académie impériale de Rouen*, 1867-68.

Beckmann, P., *Forschungen über die Quellen zur Geschichte der Jungfrau von Orleans*, Paderborn, 1872.

Berni, G., *Chronicle*.

Bloch, M., *Les Rois thaumaturges*, Paris, 1961.

Blondel, Robert, *De Reductione Normanniae*, in *Narratives of the Expulsion of the English from Normandy*, ed. Joseph Stevenson, London, 1863.

Bossuat, A., *Perrinet Gressart et François de Surienne, agents de l'Angleterre*, Paris, 1936.

Bower, Walter, *Scotichronicon*, in Q 4, 478, Paris, 1847.

B[rassart], F., *La Mission de Jeanne d'Arc*, Douai, 1881.

Bueil, J. de, *Le Jouvencel*, ed. C. Favre, 2 vols., Paris, 1887-89.

Burne, A. H., *The Agincourt War*, London, 1956.

Caffin de Mérouville, M., *Le Beau Dunois et son Temps*, Paris, 1960.

Cesbron, Chanoine, *Jeanne d'Arc et le Bas-Maine*, 2ème éd., Laval, 1929.

Champion, P., *Procès de Condamnation de Jeanne d'Arc*, 2 vols., Paris, 1920-21.

Chapoy, H., *Les Compagnons de Jeanne d'Arc*, Paris, 1897.

Chartier, Jean, *Chronique de Charles VII*, ed. Vallet de Viriville, 3 vols., Paris, 1858.

Chronicle of the Dean of Collegiate Church of Metz in Q 4, 321, Paris, 1847.

Chronique de Lorraine, in *Recueil de Documents sur l'Histoire de Lorraine*, Nancy, 1859.

Chronique de la Pucelle, ed. Vallet de Viriville, Paris, 1859.

Chroniques de Perceval de Cagny, ed. H. Moranvillé, Paris, 1902.

Chronique de Philippe de Vigneulles, ed. C. Bruneau, Metz, 1929.

Doncoeur, P. and Lanhers, Y., *Documents et Recherches relatifs à Jeanne la Pucelle,* 5 vols., Paris, 1952-1961.

Dubois, François, *Histoire du Siège d'Orléans,* 1884.

Dugdale, William, *The Baronage of England,* 2 vols., London, 1675.

Félix, Julien, *Inventaire de Pierre Surreau,* Rouen, 1892.

France, A., *The Life of Joan of Arc* (English trans.), 2 vols., London, 1908.

Frémont, *Les Payeurs d'Armes,* 1293-1870, Paris, 1906.

Gaguin, Robert, *Compendium super Francorum Gestes,* Paris, 1504. We used the copy in the Rare Book Collection of Yale University Library.

Geste des nobles François, in Vallet de Viriville's *Chronique de la Pucelle,* Paris, 1859.

Heppenstall, R., *The Fourfold Tradition,* London, 1961.

Hunt, Percival, *Fifteenth Century England,* University of Pittsburgh Press, 1962.

Jacob, E. F., *The Fifteenth Century,* Oxford, 1961.

Jarry, L., *Le Compte de l'Armée anglaise au Siège d'Orléans, 1428-29,* Orléans, 1912.

Jeny, L., and Lanéry d'Arc, P., *Jeanne d'Arc en Berry,* Paris, 1892.

Johne, T., *Chronicles of England and France,* (trans. of Froissart), London, 1839.

Journal d'un Bourgeois de Paris, ed. A. Tuétey, Paris, 1881.

Journal du Siège (Q 4, 94-202).

Knowles, David, *Great Historical Enterprises,* London, 1963.

Kurz, O., *Fakes,* London, 1948.

Laqueuille, M. le Marquis de, *Anne de Graville, Ses Poésies, son Exhérédation,* Chartres, 1858.

La Roque, G. A. de, *Histoire généalogique de la Maison d'Harcourt,* Paris, 1662.

Lasteyrie, R. de, *Jules Quicherat, sa Vie et ses Travaux,* Paris, 1883.

Les La Trémoille pendant cinq Siècles, 2 vols., Nantes, 1890-1892.

Lefèvre-Pontalis, G., *Les Sources allemandes de l'Histoire de Jeanne d'Arc, Eberhard Windecke,* Paris, 1903.

Leroy, P., *Jargeau et ses environs aux XIVe et XVe siècles,* Paris, 1893.

Lewis, C. S., *English Literature in the Sixteenth Century,* Oxford, 1959.

BOOKS MENTIONED IN THE COMMENTS

Lightbody, C., *The Judgements of Joan*, London, 1961.

Luce, S., *Jeanne d'Arc à Domremy*, Paris, 1886.

Manuscrit de Bologne, ed. André Du Bois de La Villerabel (*Les Procès de Jeanne la Pucelle*), Saint-Brieuc, 1890.

Molandon, Boucher de, *L'Armée anglaise vaincue par Jeanne d'Arc sous les Murs d'Orléans*, Orléans, 1892.

Première Expédition de Jeanne d'Arc, Orléans, 1874.

Monstrelet, Enguerrand de, *Chroniques*, ed. J. A. C. Buchon, Paris. 1836. All references are to Chapters in Book 2.

Morosini, A., *Chronique*, ed. G. Lefèvre-Pontalis, 4 vols., Paris, 1898-1902.

Mougenot, L., *Jeanne d'Arc*, Nancy, 1895.

Otway-Ruthven, J., *The King's Secretary and the Signet Office in the XV Century*, Cambridge, 1939.

Perret, P. M., *Notice Biographique sur Louis Malet de Graville, Amiral de France (144?-1516)*, Paris, 1889.

Pius II, *Commentaries of*, in *Memoirs of a Renaissance Pope*, Gragg, F. A. and Gabel, L. C., London, 1960. Miss Gragg and Miss Gabel translated and published for the first time *in extenso* in English the *Commentaries of Pius II*, in *Smith College Studies in History*, 5 issues, 1937-57.

Quicherat, J., *Procès de Condamnation et de Réhabilitation de Jeanne d'Arc*, 5 vols., Paris, 1841-49.

Register of Henry Chichele, Archbishop of Canterbury, 1414-1443, ed. E. F. Jacob, 4 vols., Oxford, 1943-47.

Relation du Greffier de La Rochelle sur Jeanne d'Arc, ed. J. Quicherat, in *Revue historique*, mai-août, 1877, 327-344.

Sarrazin, A., *Jeanne d'Arc et la Normandie*, Rouen, 1896.

Pierre Cauchon, Juge de Jeanne d'Arc, Paris, 1901.

Shakespeare, Narrative and Dramatic Sources of, ed. G. Bullough, vol. 3, London, 1960.

Stevenson, J., *Letters and Papers Illustrative of the Wars of the English in France during the Reign of Henry VI*, 2 vols., in 3 parts, London, 1861-64.

Tisset, P. and Lanhers, Y., *Procès de Condamnation de Jeanne d'Arc*, Paris, 1960.

Valois, N., *Le Pape et le Concile, 1418-1450*, 2 vols., Paris, 1909.

Vulson, Marc, sieur de La Colombière, *La Science héroïque*, Paris, 1644.

Waldman, M., *Joan of Arc*, London, 1935.

Waurin, Jean de, *Receueil des Chroniques et Anchiennes Istories de la Grant Bretaigne, a present nomme Engleterre,* ed. W. and E. Hardy, 5 vols., London, 1864-91.

William of Worcester's *Annales Rerum Anglicarum* in J. Stevenson's *Letters and Papers . . .* vol. 2, part II, pp. [743-793].

INDEX

Set in Monotype Bembo and printed by Davis & Warde, Inc.; bound by Russell-Rutter Co. Inc., New York. Book and jacket designed by Agnes L. Starrett and Thomas Pears, III, Pittsburgh. Photographs by Louis Falquet, Paris, France, except for Chinon by Valoire of Blois and frontispiece by Vic Kelly, Pittsburgh. Maps and Joan's coat of arms drawn by Mrs. John Preston, Tryon, North Carolina.

Coordinated and edited by Agnes Lynch Starrett, University of Pittsburgh Press.